TEACHING GUIDE AND RESOURCES

PEARSON

REALITY CENTRAL

GRADE 7

 PEARSON

Upper Saddle River, New Jersey • Boston, Massachusetts
Chandler, Arizona • Glenview, Illinois • Shoreview, Minnesota

ISBN-13: 978-0-13-367441-5
ISBN-10:   0-13-367441-X

1 2 3 4 5 6 7 8 9 10 12 11 10 09 08

TABLE OF CONTENTS

Philosophy and Purpose

Reality Central consists of an anthology of accessible nonfiction articles on edgy and often debatable topics for struggling readers in grades 6 through 10. The *Real World Writing Journal* and the *Teaching Guide and Resources* are companions to the student anthologies. The topics in the student anthology are relevant to students' experiences and serve as motivating factors for reading and discussion.

Program Materials

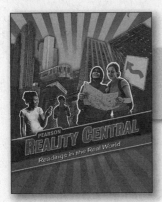

The *Reality Central* student anthology brings real-life topics to readers with scaffolded support throughout each lesson.

The *Real World Writing Journal* supports your students as they write about topics related to the student anthology and deeply explore vocabulary words. A handbook of grammar, usage, and mechanics is a ready reference for student writers and a practice tool to lift each writer's skills.

The *Teaching Guide and Resources* provides a systematic and explicit approach to teaching with the student anthology and writing journal. Innovative think-alouds, teaching tips, and suggestions for making the content accessible for all readers allow you to differentiate instruction and reach learners of varying proficiency levels.

Who benefits from *Reality Central*?

The materials in *Reality Central* are suitable for work with the whole class, but they are specially crafted for readers who may need extra support.

Struggling Readers

All components of *Reality Central* provide practice and support for struggling readers by addressing the following critical elements:

- **Vocabulary Development** Multiple exposure to content and academic vocabulary is developed throughout the anthology articles. Each unit focuses on a small number of crucial words, repeating words in various forms throughout the unit. The *Real World Writing Journal* provides opportunities for further practice in various contexts.

- **Connection to Background Knowledge** Each article begins with a Real-Life Connection that allows students to connect what they already know with what they will learn.

- **Targeted Writing Instruction** Writing instruction that includes pre-writing, drafting, and revision is explicit and systematic, allowing students to take gradual ownership of the entire writing process.

- **Discussion** Numerous opportunities for discussion support the reading and provide practice in critical thinking and oral language skills.

English Learners

The student anthology in *Reality Central* is appropriate not only for struggling readers, but also for ELs (English Learners). Pedagogy important for ELs included in *Reality Central* includes:

- **Pre-reading Support** A controlled number of vocabulary words are systematically introduced before reading. Students connect what they already know to article topics. In some cases, topics may be new to students. Relevant background information is provided to help readers get the most out of the articles.

THE HIGH COST OF GRAFFITI		
Name of City	Population in 2006	Amount Spent (in $)
San Jose, California	1,000,000	2,000,000
Pittsburgh, Pennsylvania	300,000	350,000
Omaha, Nebraska	400,000	100,000
Denver, Colorado	550,000	1,000,000
Milwaukee, Wisconsin	550,000	1,000,000
Chicago, Illinois	2,800,000	6,500,000

Information is from Graffitihurts.org.

- **Support During Reading** Selections have been carefully written at Lexile levels appropriate for ELs. In addition, articles include limited use of idioms and other language that may be difficult for ELs. Graphic sources in the articles provide other methods for students to access information.

- **Post-reading Support** Comprehension of text is scaffolded by beginning with literal questions after reading. These questions support students as they "find it on the page." As students' confidence and ability to navigate text grow, questions invite them to use their critical thinking and problem-solving skills.

What features are important to *Reality Central*?

Big Questions anchor units.

- A Big Question appears on the unit opener for each unit. Opening activities use the Big Question as an anchor for the other activities in the unit.
- Each article has its own Big Question, carefully related to the Unit Big Question.
- A closing activity allows for students to solidify their thinking about the Big Questions. In a creative format, such as a debate, television show, or bulletin board, students demonstrate the depth of their understanding of the Big Question.

Careful consideration of leveling cultivates students' success.

- Articles are typically one to two reading levels below the targeted grade-level audience.
- The articles are written with accessible language in a student-friendly tone.
- Visuals such as graphs and charts support students' informational literacy.

Multiple readings foster growth in skills.

- Lesson plans outline a multiple-reading strategy that builds fluency and the use of comprehension strategies.
- On a first reading, the teacher may read to students and guide their thinking.
- On repeated readings, students own the reading process by looking for clues that help them answer questions.
- As students delve into writing, they are encouraged to revisit the article for details that support their ideas.

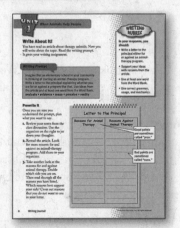

Opportunities for direct instruction in writing, vocabulary, and grammar lift students' achievement.

- Writing instruction follows a mediated approach, in which students receive instruction in all phases of the writing process. Modeling by the teacher enhances student understanding.
- Direct instruction in vocabulary focuses on the idea that multiple exposures to words in various contexts provide not just familiarity, but the ability to use a growing vocabulary.
- A handbook of grammar, usage, and mechanics provides exercises that focus on "real-life" writings. The handbook approach treats editing not as a "chore," but as a strategy.

Reality Central **Student Anthology**

Unit Opener

❶ Use the illustration to engage students and prompt their thinking.

❷ Set the stage and provide a purpose for reading by sharing the Big Question.

The teaching plan includes suggestions for creating a visual anchor for the unit focused on the Big Question.

Article

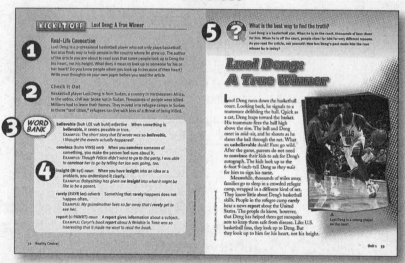

❶ Use the Real-Life Connection to link the article topic to students' experiences, providing a connection and engaging readers.

❷ Read the Check It Out features with students to share information that they will need to access ideas in the text.

❸ Introduce the Word Bank. Many of these words appear multiple times throughout the unit, introducing a controlled vocabulary.

❹ Highlight the example section in the Word Bank to put each word into a meaningful context for students.

❺ Read through the introduction with students to prompt their thinking about the topic and the Article Big Question. Discuss how the Article Big Question and the Unit Big Question are connected.

Article

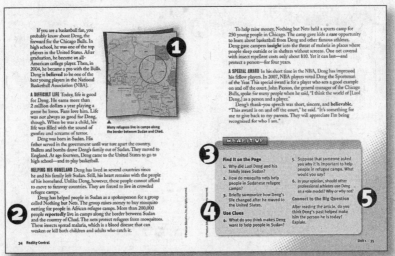

❶ Draw attention to graphics, charts, and other visuals to boost students' nonfiction literacy skills.

❷ Point out the boldface vocabulary words. These words are variations of the Word Bank words.

❸ Use the "Find It on the Page" questions to key students directly to lesson content.

❹ Prompt deeper thinking with the "Use Clues" questions after a second reading.

❺ Bring students back to the Big Question to provide closure.

Unit Closer

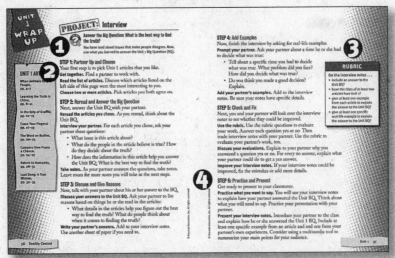

❶ Introduce the product students will create.

❷ Follow the instructions to guide students in creating a product that answers the Unit Big Question and uses information from the articles.

❸ Prompt students to use the rubric in order to assess and make changes to their work.

❹ Encourage students to share their work.

Reality Central **Real World Writing Journal**

Write About It!

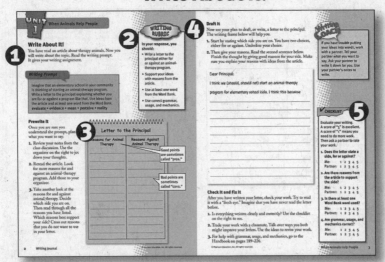

① Introduce the topic with the writing prompt.

② Point out the rubric before students begin to write to help them focus their writing goals.

③ Model how to use the graphic organizer. Assist students as they gather their thoughts.

④ Prompt students to use a mediated approach for their writing as they follow the steps in organizing their finished work.

⑤ Draw attention to the checklist as a way for students to evaluate—and then to make changes—to improve their writing.

Vocabulary Workshop

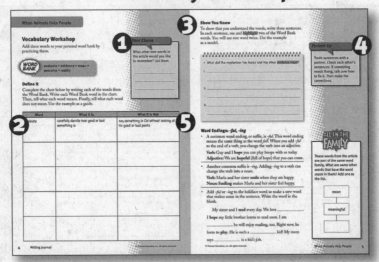

① After revisiting the Word Bank words, encourage students to record other words from the article. These words can be recorded in the personal word bank in the back of the journal.

② Help students use words in various contexts as they complete graphic organizers.

③ Encourage students to demonstrate their understanding using the Show You Know activities.

④ Pair students and use the Partner Up suggestions to guide their work.

⑤ A culminating activity allows students to use word parts, sort words, or investigate multiple-meaning words.

Grammar, Usage, and Mechanics Handbook

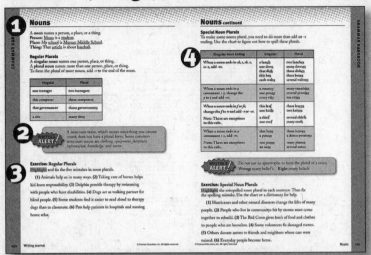

1 Use the introduction to provide direct instruction.

2 Point out the Writer's Alerts, demonstrating how these alerts help students avoid common mistakes.

3 Discuss the exercises, which provide explicit strategy practice.

4 Draw attention to the charts that organize useful information about grammar, usage, and mechanics for an at-a-glance reference.

Checklist and Word Bank

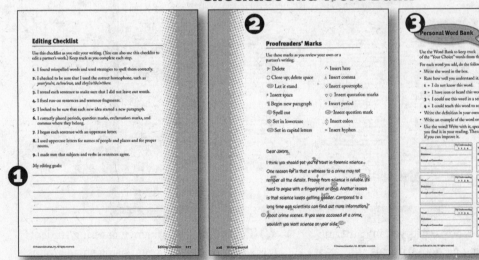
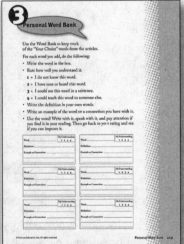

1 Encourage students to add their own goals to an editing checklist.

2 Demonstrate how to use proofreaders' marks to perform a thorough edit and revision to create a polished piece of writing.

3 Have students add the "Your Choice" words to the personal word bank. Encourage them to rate their knowledge, use the words, and then rate their knowledge again.

Reality Central **Teaching Guide and Resources**

Unit Opener Lesson

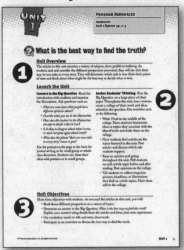

❶ Set the stage for the unit by discussing the unit opener in the anthology.

❷ Begin a visual anchor to guide students' thinking as they read the unit selections.

❸ State objectives for the unit to prepare students for reading, writing, and discussion.

Article Lesson: Student Anthology and Writing Journal

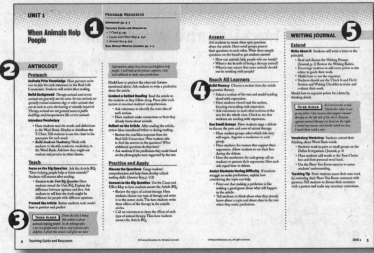

❶ The Resources box assists you in gathering and organizing needed materials.

❷ Each part of the lesson includes directions to help your students get the most out of the student anthology articles.

❸ Think Alouds prompt explicit modeling. Modeling gives a window to your thinking as students follow your lead.

❹ Tips for building fluency, assisting students who are struggling, and using small groups allow you to reach all your learners.

❺ Teaching Tips and Think Alouds provide deeper instruction for the *Real World Writing Journal*.

Unit Closer Lesson

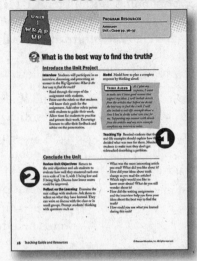

1 Use the Think Aloud and Teaching Tip to deepen the instruction of the unit closer activity.

2 Wrap up the visual anchor for the unit and link it back to the Big Question to bring the unit to a close.

Additional Instructional Support

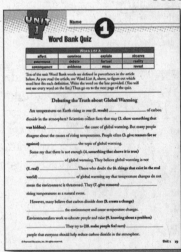

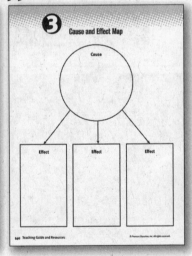

1 The Word Bank Quiz assesses students' understanding of vocabulary by providing context clues in a passage.

2 Answer Keys are provided for the student anthology questions, vocabulary exercises from the *Real World Writing Journal*, the unit Word Bank Quiz, and the Grammar, Usage, and Mechanics Handbook.

3 Graphic organizers key into instruction in comprehension and vocabulary, allow students to gather thoughts about Big Questions, and assist students who need to make further connections.

Correlations to Prentice Hall *Literature*

Each unit in *Reality Central* has a corresponding unit in Prentice Hall *Literature*. The units in both anthologies have identical Big Questions. Each selection in the *Reality Central* Student Anthology is linked to a reading selection in Prentice Hall *Literature*. Individual selections may be linked by topic or by theme.

As a supplement to Prentice Hall *Literature*, *Reality Central* allows you to:

- build students' background knowledge of a topic with related nonfiction.
- support struggling readers by presenting a related selection at a reading level that matches students' levels of proficiency.
- explore the various treatments of ideas and themes across genres.

- expand students' strategy use to multiple genres with varying text features.
- allow students multiple opportunities to think about the Big Questions as they read selections in different genres with different treatments of topics and themes.
- provide multiple exposure to vocabulary words in different contexts.

Reality Central can be used effectively on its own, but it also provides strong links to Prentice Hall *Literature*.

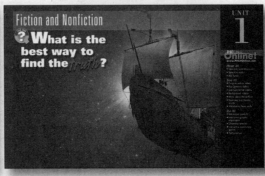

With identical Big Questions, both resources allow for exploration across genres and topics.

Strong links between selections allow *Reality Central* to be used in conjunction with Prentice Hall *Literature*.

Unit 1: How do we decide what is true?

Reality Central Title	Page	Prentice Hall Literature Title	Page
When Animals Help People	4–7	Papa's Parrot	26
Learning the Truth in China	8–11	MK	34
In the Grip of Graffiti	12–15	From An American Childhood	52
Cross Your Fingers!	16–19	The Luckiest Time of All	62
The Word on Bullies	20–23	All Summer in a Day	102
Campers Give Peace a Chance	24–27	Suzy and Leah	114
Return to Humanity	28–31	My First Free Summer	132
Luol Deng: A True Winner	32–35	Angela's Ashes	140

Unit 2: Is conflict always bad?

Reality Central Title	Page	Prentice Hall Literature Title	Page
Athletes as Role Models	40–43	The Bear Boy	220
Coyotes on the Go	44–47	Rikki-tikki-tavi	228
Moms and Dads in the Military	48–51	from Letters from Rifka	252
Sports Parents	52–55	Two Kinds	260
The Kindness of Kin	56–59	The Third Wish	312
Sister Champions	60–63	Amigo Brothers	322
Two Views of the Zoo	64–67	Zoo	340
Either Too Young or Too Old	68–71	Ribbons	346

Unit 3: What is important to know?

Reality Central Title	Page	Prentice Hall Literature Title	Page
Travel to Mars	76–79	Life Without Gravity	424
Look Who's Talking	80–83	Conversational Ballgames	432
Making Sport of Tradition	84–87	I Am a Native North American	444
In Your Dreams	88–91	Volar: To Fly	452
The Titans Remember	92–95	All Together Now	494
The Price of Discovery	96–99	The Eternal Frontier	500
Someone Has to Do It	100–103	The Real Story of a Cowboy's Life	510
Have No Fear	104–107	Rattlesnake Hunt	518

Unit 4: Do we need words to communicate well?

Reality Central Title	Page	Prentice Hall *Literature* Title	Page
Thinking of You	112–115	The Rider Seal Haiku	586, 588, 590
Word on the Wire	116–119	Winter Forysthia Haiku	594, 595, 596
A Show of Strength	120–123	Life Loo-wit The Courage That My Mother Had	604, 606, 608
The Big Money	124–127	Mother to Son The Village Blacksmith Fog	612, 614, 616
Pay Days	128–131	Sarah Cynthia One Weather	650, 652, 654
The Music Mix	132–135	Full Fathom Five Train Tune Onomatopoeia	658, 659, 660
Follow Your Star	136–139	Annabel Lee Martin Luther King I'm Nobody	668, 670, 672
The Age Factor	140–143	Jim Father William Stopping By Woods	676, 678, 682

Unit 5: How do we decide what is true?

Reality Central Title	Page	Prentice Hall *Literature* Title	Page
How Attitude Helps	148–151	A Christmas Carol: Act 1	740
Happiness: A Two-Way Street?	152–155	A Christmas Carol: Act 1	740
Called Out	156–159	A Christmas Carol: Act 2	775
Pushing Buttons	160–163	The Monsters Are Due on Maple Street	834

Unit 6: How much do our communities shape us?

Reality Central Title	Page	Prentice Hall *Literature* Title	Page
The Great Dress Debate	168–171	Icarus and Daedalus	916
Commanding the Weather	172–175	Demeter and Persephone	924
Restoring Cities from the Ground Up	176–179	Tenochtilan: Inside the Aztec Capital	938
What It Takes to Lead	180–183	Popcatepetl and Ixtlaccihuatl	946
Rebuilding Communities	184–187	Sun and Moon in a Box	992
The Irresistible Urban Myth	188–191	How the Snake Got Poison	1000
The Ripple Effect	192–195	The People Could Fly	1010
Trickster Appeal—Revealed!	196–199	All Stories Are Anansi's	1018

Supporting Struggling Readers

The materials in *Reality Central* are designed especially with struggling readers in mind. As you read through the lessons in the *Teaching Guide and Resources*, you will notice strategies designed to allow students to improve their comprehension and build fluency. Small group activities will engage readers and prompt deeper thinking.

There are many strategies that encourage and support vocabulary development. The following are suggestions you may want to use or adapt for your students. The *Reality Central Teaching Guide and Resources* use many of these activities, supporting the growth of your readers.

Read aloud to students.

Read aloud to students on a "first run" of the text. Your readaloud serves multiple purposes. You model fluent reading for students, focusing on correct phrasing, attention to punctuation, emphasizing meaning, and so on. Use your readaloud as a time to model your use of reading strategies. Provide a window into your thinking, telling students what you are doing before you read the text and pausing occasionally to model strategy use. Your thinkaloud should be "in the moment," showing the strategies that you are using as a proficient reader. You do not, for example, want to say, "Look, I'm summarizing now." Instead, summarize naturally, showing students that strategies are helpful for navigating text, not simply "one more thing to do."

Model by thinking aloud.

Pause to "fix up" as you go so that students see first-hand what good readers do when they encounter unknown words or difficult ideas. Some of the many strategies you might model in a think aloud include:

- *figuring out word meanings*
- *applying background knowledge to text*
- *making predictions based on text features*
- *changing predictions during reading*
- *thinking about opinions and reactions*
- *summarizing*
- *differentiating between important ideas and "nice to know"*
- *making mental pictures*
- *rereading, reading on*

Focus on pre-reading tasks.

With the articles in *Reality Central*, the pre-reading process can include examining graphics, captions, pull-out quotes, headings, and so on. Share a routine for pre-reading:

- **Read the title:** What clues does it give you about the topic and the author's focus?
- **Read the introduction:** The introduction is a lead-in. What does it tell you about the rest of the article?
- **Read the boldface headings:** The heads are labels for the sections. Can you predict what the article might be about? Can you set purposes for reading?
- **Look for boldface words:** Word Bank Words are boldface in the articles. What do these words tell you about the content of the article?
- **Look over visual aids:** *Reality Central* articles showcase photographs, charts, and graphs. What information can you glean from these graphic sources?
- **Read through the questions at the end:** How does reading these questions help you set purposes for reading?

Use graphic organizers.

Graphic organizers help students organize ideas before, during, and after reading. Use the graphic organizers on pages 140-157 of this resource as starting points for assisting your students with exploring Big Questions and thinking more deeply about their comprehension. A Table of Contents on page 139 describes each graphic organizer and offers hints on how each might be used with your students.

Teach fix-up strategies.

Struggling readers often work through the text with the idea of getting to the end. Work with students to have them monitor their thinking and "fix-up" their problems.

As students read, they can mark trouble spots with sticky notes. As students revisit or navigate through parts of the text that confuse them, offer these strategies as tools:

Make a Prediction: Think about what is coming next to set purposes for reading and look for "answers."

Make a Connection: Think about what you already know to better understand what you are reading.

Ask Questions: Stop and ask questions as you read. You may or may not find the answers in the text, but you are setting the stage for purposeful reading.

Stop and Think About What You Have Read: Rather than read on, stop and think. What do you already know about this? What have you learned so far? What do you still wonder about?

Adjust Your Rate: Adjust the reading rate depending on how hard the material is to read, what you already know about it, and the purpose you have for reading.

Visualize: Create images in your head that will help you make sense of the words on the page.

Retell: Can you retell the main ideas in your own words and not the author's words? Tell a partner about what you have read. See if you include all the important words.

Focus on fluency.

The lessons in the *Teaching Guide and Resources* include strategies for building fluency with your readers. Strategies such as these help students focus on all aspects of fluency—speed, accuracy, and expression.

Echo Reading You read a portion of the text, modeling phrasing, accuracy, and so on. Then students, individually or in small groups, echo after you. You can pair readers for this activity.

Choral Reading Choral reading is reading done in a group, with or without your lead. Students should choral read only text that is familiar to them.

Partner Reading Students read aloud for each other as partners listen and perhaps take notes. They offer tips to partners on the reading. Carefully model this process and how to offer feedback beyond "good job"!

Tape Recordings Have students tape record their readings. They can listen, identify areas for improvement, and read again to assess their growth. You can also save tape recordings for "readalongs."

Supporting Struggling Writers

All writers, even proficient ones, struggle at times during the writing process. Writing instruction in *Reality Central* provides scaffolds for students who need them, with the goal of eventually removing supports as writers gain confidence and proficiency.

There are many strategies that encourage and support development of struggling writers. The following are suggestions you may want to use or adapt for your students. The *Reality Central Real World Writing Journal* uses many of these activities, supporting the growth of your writers.

Help students diagnose their own difficulties.

Remind students that all writers struggle sometimes, and one strategy to become more proficient at writing is to figure out the exact causes of writing problems. Prompt writers with questions such as:

- Do you understand the writing form and what your product should look like?
- Do you understand the topic well enough to write about it? If not, what can you do to learn more?
- What needs to be clearer in the directions?
- Do you know how to begin the piece?

Once you start asking questions focused on the writing process and product, you'll begin to know which questions are best for prompting which students. Soon, students will begin to identify their own problems.

Hold writing conferences.

Confer often with individuals as they write. Conferences can be a "formal" scheduled time, but consider incorporating on-the-run assessment. Use the information you gather to pinpoint individual students' needs as you work with them. If a small group of students face the same problem with their writing, pull them together for a mini lesson focused on their particular challenge, such as not knowing how to write a powerful beginning. Use these informal conferences as a way to assist with particular problems that you diagnose rather than meeting at a "set time."

Use graphic organizers.

Organizers can help students as they are forming their ideas for writing. Students can also use graphic organizers as they write, moving ideas from one place to another, trying out different combinations of ideas, and soon. Have students' graphic organizers on hand as you conference with them, pointing out how they might better organize or beef up their writing. The graphic organizers on pages 140–157 of this resource provide starting points for writers. The *Reality Central Real World Writing Journal* provides a graphic organizer for each writing assignment, but students may find other organizers helpful as well.

Provide writing models.

Provide two types of models for students:

Teacher Models Model writing for students. When you model, do the writing yourself. As students gain more proficiency, you can invite them to share their ideas for writing and make the process more interactive; but on a first modeling, explicitly share your thinking as you write. Write the way that you would write, rather than writing as a student would write, to show students how to lift their writing to the next level. As you create modeled writing pieces, save them for students' reference in the future.

Student Models Displaying and discussing student models is one way to showcase great work, but those student models also can help students see what they are trying to accomplish. You might give small groups student models (removing student identifiers or using pieces from past classes) and ask groups to assess those models. They can identify the positive points of the writing they examine and discuss how to incorporate those traits into their own pieces of writing.

Build background.

Beginning a writing piece "cold" is difficult even for the most seasoned writers. Provide background for students before they write to help them become more comfortable with the writing process and assignment. Use ideas such as the following:

- Model how to begin the process with graphic organizers.
- Prompt discussion in pairs, small groups, or with the whole class.
- Share readings, images, or video about writing topics.
- Have students "quick write," not as a final product, but to have ideas to begin their writing.

Provide tools for writers.

Steep your classroom in tools that students that can use to elevate their writing:

- Show students self-assessment tools and checklists and model their use. You can use the tools in the back of this resource or devise your own (or have students devise them).
- Provide checklists such as the editing checklist and proofreaders' marks in the *Reality Central Real World Writing Journal*. Having students design checklists helps them focus on the traits of good writing.
- Create posters as visual reminders, such as appropriate vocabulary to use for different types of writing.
- Have students create word banks of words useful for different types of writing. Students, for example, could work with you to create a word bank of transitions or a word bank of words that are effective in persuasive writing.

Supporting Vocabulary Development

Vocabulary instruction has a profound effect on students' comprehension of academic content. Systematic instruction of vocabulary words allows students to make important gains in background knowledge and approach text with a higher probability of understanding important ideas.

Vocabulary instruction in *Reality Central* focuses on words that students will see frequently, academic vocabulary, and words that may be difficult. Vocabulary words are provided in several different forms in the articles in the student anthology.

In general, you can help support students' vocabulary development by:

- activating prior knowledge about vocabulary words.
- defining words in multiple contexts.
- assisting students in using context clues to determine word meanings.
- explicitly teaching word parts (prefixes, roots, and suffixes) as clues to word meaning.
- providing opportunities for students to integrate new vocabulary into their speaking and writing.
- giving multiple exposures to new words.
- focusing on a small number of important words.
- relating words to concepts to increase depth of content knowledge.

There are many strategies that encourage and support vocabulary development. The following are suggestions you may want to use or adapt for your students.

Introduce and activate the meanings of words.

When you introduce word meaning, provide meaningful real-life context.

EXAMPLE

Endurance is the ability to handle pain or hardship for a long time. We hear about people who have endurance and tasks that require it. Think about athletes who run marathons. Running a marathon might be painful after a while. It takes a lot of endurance to run for so long. Can you think of someone who has shown a lot of endurance, who was able to put up with hardship or pain? In what situations is endurance useful?

Provide a sentence completion activity.

Provide a sentence frame that encourages students to stretch their thinking about vocabulary words. As students complete these sentences, you can further clarify word meanings.

EXAMPLE

Restrict: to limit; to confine; to control
Some things that I know about that are restricted are _____

Present cloze activities.

Present words in different contexts by writing sentences that use the words, then removing the words and leaving "blanks" in the sentences for students to fill in. Encourage discussion as students begin filling in the blanks, especially if more than one word might make sense.

A paragraph cloze provides an opportunity for students to practice using context. Model for students how to skip over choices that are difficult, cross out words as they are used, and "try out" possibilities to find the best fit. Guide students with questions such as "Is this the only word that fits?" and "What makes this choice the best?"

Provide multiple ways for students to define and explore words graphically.

Graphic organizers prompt students to think about and describe the meanings of words and concepts. Use the graphic organizers throughout the *Real World Writing Journal* and on pages 140–157 of this resource as starting points for assisting your students with exploration of vocabulary words. Graphic organizers might include such elements as definitions, characteristics, examples, non-examples, similar words, and so on.

Use word analogy exercises.

Students explain the relationship between words and use that relationship to create new pairs.

Types of analogies include:

Part to whole:	bulb : flashlight :: petal : flower
Person to situation:	fisherman : rod :: artist : brush
Synonym:	graceful : elegant :: loud : noisy
Antonym:	graceful : clumsy :: loud : quiet
Geography:	Chicago : Illinois :: Los Angeles : California
Measurement:	inch: foot :: centimeter : meter

Sort words.

Word sorting is a simple activity for students to do independently or in groups. You can provide categories to students and then ask students to sort vocabulary words into these categories, such as parts of speech. Alternatively, provide students a list of words and challenge them to sort these words into categories after discerning the common features and describing the categories.

What is the best way to find the truth?

Unit Overview

The articles in this unit examine a variety of subjects, from graffiti to bullying. As students read and consider the different perspectives presented, they will see that there may be two sides to every story. They will determine which side is true from their points of view and think about what might be the best way to decide what is true.

Launch the Unit

Connect to the Big Question Read the introduction with students and examine the illustrations. Ask questions such as:

- *What are some issues that people have different opinions about?*
- *Describe what you see in the illustration.*
- *How does the student in the illustration attempt to decide what is true?*
- *Is it okay to disagree about what is true, or must everyone agree about truth?*
- *What does the phrase "there are two sides to every story" mean to you?*

Use the prompt on the page as the basis for journal writing or for small group or whole class discussion. Students can share their ideas with partners or in small groups.

Anchor Students' Thinking Post the Big Question on a large piece of chart paper. Throughout the unit, have students create a collage of their work and ideas related to the question. Use activities such as the following:

- Write *Truth* in the middle of the collage. Have students brainstorm ideas or topics they associate with truth and write them on the collage.
- Have students find articles on the topics featured in the unit. Post articles and discuss which side students support.
- Keep an opinion poll going throughout the unit. Poll students on each article topic before and after reading. Post opinions on the collage.
- Tell students to collect magazine pictures, headlines, or illustrations they find on article topics. Have them add to the collage.

Unit Objectives

Share these objectives with students. As you read the articles in this unit, you will:

- Read about different perspectives on a variety of topics.
- Determine an answer to the Big Question: *What is the best way to find the truth?* Explain your answers using details from the articles and from your own experiences.
- Use vocabulary words to talk and write about truth.
- Participate in an interview to discuss the best way to find the truth.

When Animals Help People

PROGRAM RESOURCES

ANTHOLOGY pp. 4–7

TEACHING GUIDE AND RESOURCES
- T-Chart **p. 151**
- Cause and Effect Map **p. 140**
- Answer Key **p. 112**

REAL WORLD WRITING JOURNAL pp. 2–5

ANTHOLOGY

Preteach

Activate Prior Knowledge Have partners write *true* or *false* for each statement in the Real-Life Connection. Students will revisit after reading.

Build Background *Therapy animals and service animals are generally not the same. Service animals are specially trained assistance dogs or other animals that can do tasks to assist the hearing or visually impaired. Therapy animals are not granted access to public buildings and transportation like service animals.*

Introduce Vocabulary

- Have students read the words and definitions in the Word Bank. Display or distribute the T-Chart. Tell students to use the chart to list synonyms for each word.
- *Build Academic Vocabulary* Work with students to identify academic vocabulary in the Word Bank. Ask how they might use *evaluate* and *perceive* in other classes.

Teach

Focus on the Big Question Ask the Article BQ, "Does helping people help or harm animals?" Students will answer after reading.

- *Connect to the Unit Big Question* Have students reread the Unit BQ. Explain the difference between opinion and fact. Ask students to tell how the truth might be different for people with different opinions.

Preread the Article Before students read, model how to preview and predict:

> **THINK ALOUD** *From the title I know this article is about animals helping people. In the photographs I see two people and a horse, and a picture of a dolphin. I think this article will give me more information about how horses and dolphins help people. I will look at the picture, captions, title, and subheads to make more predictions.*

Model how to preview the other text features mentioned above. Ask students to write a prediction about the article.

Conduct a Guided Reading Read the article to the students as they follow along. Pause after each section to monitor students' comprehension.

- Ask volunteers to identify the main idea of each section.
- Have students make connections to facts they already know about animals.

Reflect on the Article After reading the article, review ideas introduced before or during reading.

- Review the true/false responses from the Real-Life Connection. Were students able to find the answers to the questions? What additional questions do they have?
- Ask students if the predictions they made based on the photographs were supported by the text.

Practice and Apply

Discuss the Questions Gauge students' comprehension and help them develop critical reading skills. (Answer Key, p. 112)

Connect to the Big Question Use the Cause and Effect Map to have students answer the Article BQ.

- Review the types of animal therapy. Have students choose one type of therapy and write it in the center circle. The have students write three effects of the therapy in the outside circles.
- Call on volunteers to share the effects of each type of animal therapy. Then have students answer the Article BQ.

Assess

Ask students to create three quiz questions about the article. Have small groups present their questions to each other. Write these sample questions on the board to get students started:

- How can animals help people who are lonely?
- What is the benefit of being a therapy animal?
- What is one reason that some animals should not be working with people?

Reach All Learners

Build Fluency Choose a section from the article to practice fluency.

- Select a section of the text and model reading aloud with expression.
- Have students choral read the section, focusing on reading with expression.
- Ask volunteers to read other sections of the text for the whole class. Check to see that students are reading with expression.

Use Small Groups Have students stage a debate to discuss the pros and cons of animal therapy.

- Have student groups select which side they will argue. Appoint a moderator to each group.
- Have students list reasons that support their arguments. Allow students to use their lists during the debate.
- Have the moderator for each group call on students to present their arguments. Give each side equal time to debate.

Assist Students Having Difficulty If students struggle to make predictions, explain how considering the topic can help.

- Point out that making a prediction is like making a good guess about what will happen in the article.
- Tell students to think about what they already know about a topic and about clues in the text when they make predictions.

WRITING JOURNAL

Extend

Write About It Students will write a letter to the principal.

- Read and discuss the Writing Prompt. (Journal, p. 2) Review the Writing Rubric.
- Encourage students to add more points to the rubric to guide their work.
- Model how to use the organizer.
- Students should use the Check It and Fix It Section and Writing Checklist to revise and evaluate their work.

Model how to organize points for a letter by thinking aloud:

> **THINK ALOUD** *As I review the article, I find other ideas to use in my letter. I list reasons that support animal therapy on the left side of the chart. Reasons against animal therapy are listed on the right. I reread my reasons and decide which are best. I mark them with a star.*

Vocabulary Workshop Students extend their thinking about Word Bank words.

- Students work in pairs or small groups on the Define It organizer. (Journal, p. 4)
- Have students add words to the Your Choice box and their personal word bank.
- Use the Show You Know exercise to assess students' understanding.

Teaching Tip Have students assess their own work by reviewing their Show You Know sentences with partners. Tell students to discuss their sentences with a partner and make any necessary corrections.

Learning the Truth in China

PROGRAM RESOURCES

ANTHOLOGY pp. 8–11

TEACHING GUIDE AND RESOURCES
- Main Idea Map **p. 146**
- T-Chart **p. 151**
- Answer Key **p. 112**

REAL WORLD WRITING JOURNAL pp. 6–9

ANTHOLOGY

Preteach

Activate Prior Knowledge Have students copy and complete the Real-Life Connection chart independently. Students will revisit after reading.

Build Background *China, Iran, and Vietnam are a few countries that control the information people are allowed to find on the Internet. The governments of these countries block information they consider sensitive or controversial.*

Introduce Vocabulary

- Have students scan the article to find the sentences with boldface vocabulary words. Ask volunteers to read these sentences aloud.
- Have students work in pairs to write a definition in their own words for each word.
- *Build Academic Vocabulary* Write the academic vocabulary words on the board. Discuss with students how they might use *awareness* and *explain* in social studies.

Teach

Focus on the Big Question Ask the Article BQ, "How does the country in which you live affect the information that you can find?" Students will answer this question after reading.

- *Connect to the Unit Big Question* Write the Unit and Article BQs on the board. Have students discuss the connection between finding truth and finding information.

Preread the Article Before students read, model how to preview the subtitles to make predictions:

> **THINK ALOUD** *The subtitles are in bold at the top of each section. "Censoring the Internet," "Living with Censorship," and "Looking Forward" are the subtitles. I predict that the first section will explain that people in certain places do not have access to information because other people decide they cannot see it.*

Ask students to write a prediction about the article. Have students keep their predictions so they can revisit them after reading the article.

Conduct a Guided Reading Read the article to students as they follow along. Pause after each section to monitor students' comprehension.

- Display or distribute the Main Idea Map.
- Have students fill in the graphic organizer during a second reading of the article.

Reflect on the Article After reading the article, review ideas introduced before or during reading.

- Have students review their Real-Life Connection responses. Ask volunteers to share what they learned from the article.
- Ask students to review their predictions. Were they accurate?

Practice and Apply

Discuss the Questions Gauge students' comprehension and help them develop critical reading skills. (Answer Key, p. 112)

Connect to the Big Question Have students use the T-Chart to organize ideas.

- Have students write the Article BQ on their organizers. Then have students list the differences between finding information in the United States and China.
- Tell students to review their ideas and reread the Article BQ. Then ask volunteers to volunteer answers based on the differences they have listed.

Assess

Tell students to imagine they will interview a student who lives in China. Have students work with partners to write four questions they would like to ask the student about censorship. Tell students that their questions must reflect what they have learned from the article.

Reach All Learners

Build Fluency Choose a section from the article for an Echo Reading.

- Tell students to focus on pausing at appropriate punctuation as they read aloud.
- Have students read a section aloud to partners, pausing at appropriate punctuation. Then have partners repeat the process.
- Have students revisit the paragraph they read aloud, pointing out the punctuation that indicates a reader should pause.

Use Small Groups Use a think/pair/share activity for one of the Use Clues questions.

- Organize students into small groups and assign each group a question from the Use Clues section.
- Have students think/pair/share. Tell students to think about how they would answer the question and then pair up with a group member to discuss their answer.
- Ask volunteers from each group to share their ideas with the class.

Assist Students Having Difficulty If students struggle to compare and contrast the Internet in the United States with the Internet in China, have them think about their own Internet use.

- Tell students to list the ways they use the Internet at home and at school.
- Have students circle words that might be censored if they were in China. Allow students to refer to the article for ideas.

WRITING JOURNAL

Extend

Write About It Students will write an article for the school newspaper.

- Read and discuss the Writing Prompt. (Journal, p. 6) Review the Writing Rubric.
- Encourage students to add more points to the rubric to guide their work.
- Model how to use the organizer.
- Students should use the Check It and Fix It Section and Writing Checklist to revise and evaluate their work.

Model how to write a title by thinking aloud:

THINK ALOUD *A title grabs the reader's attention and summarizes what the article is about. What if I start with "The Internet"? That does not say much or grab interest. I will try again: "Censorship Unfair on the 'Net." That is better. It gives information to readers.*

Vocabulary Workshop Students extend their thinking about Word Bank words.

- Students work in pairs or small groups on the Define It organizer. (Journal, p. 8)
- Have students add words to the Your Choice box and their personal word bank.
- Use the Show You Know exercise to assess students' understanding.

Teaching Tip Have the class brainstorm additional words ending in -*ness*. List words on the board and challenge partners to write a short paragraph using some of the words in context.

UNIT 1

In the Grip of Graffiti

PROGRAM RESOURCES

ANTHOLOGY pp. 12–15

TEACHING GUIDE AND RESOURCES
- Comic Strip Organizer **p. 141**
- Problem and Solution Map **p. 149**
- Answer Key **p. 113**

REAL WORLD WRITING JOURNAL pp. 10–13

ANTHOLOGY

Preteach

Activate Prior Knowledge Have students copy and complete the word web on graffiti. Students will revisit their webs after reading.

Build Background *Some cities must spend millions of dollars each year removing graffiti from public buildings and walls. The United States, however, is not the only country that has problems with graffiti. Cities in countries such as Northern Ireland, England, and France also spend thousands on clean-up.*

Introduce Vocabulary

- Read aloud the sentences from the article in which boldface vocabulary words appear. Discuss what each word means in context.
- Display or distribute the Comic Strip Organizer. Have students select three words from the Word Bank to illustrate.
- *Build Academic Vocabulary* Write the academic vocabulary words *conclude, debate, evaluate,* and *perceive* on index cards. Divide students into small groups and distribute a card to each. Have groups explain how they might use the word in another subject.

Teach

Focus on the Big Question Ask the Article BQ, "Is graffiti art, or is it damage to property?" Students will answer this question after reading.

- *Connect to the Unit Big Question* Write the Unit and Article BQs on the board. Discuss with students how different opinions might result in different answers to the questions.

Preread the Article Before students read, model how to preview text features and make predictions:

| THINK ALOUD | *I read the title and scan the article for text features. I wonder who or what is "in the grip" of this problem. The chart on p. 14 shows the population of some major cities and how much each spends on graffiti removal. I think the article will tell me how some cities are affected by graffiti and how they are solving the problem.* |

Ask students to scan the article for other text features and write a prediction about the article.

Conduct a Guided Reading Read the article to students as they follow along. Pause after each section to monitor students' comprehension.

- Display or distribute the Problem and Solution Map.
- Have students take notes on the problem of graffiti as they read.

Reflect on the Article After reading the article, review ideas introduced before or during reading.

- Have students revisit the predictions they made before reading. Was the prediction proved true? Why or why not?
- Ask volunteers to share facts about graffiti removal they learned from the article.

Practice and Apply

Discuss the Questions Gauge students' comprehension and help them develop critical reading skills. (Answer Key, p. 113)

Connect to the Big Question Refocus students' attention on the Article BQ.

- Have groups discuss their opinions of graffiti and take a poll. Students can record how many believe graffiti is art.
- Then ask students to imagine they own property that was "tagged." Have students propose solutions to the problem.

Assess

Have students create a Learning Log for you to review. Students should answer these questions:

- What was your opinion about graffiti before reading the article?
- What did you learn about graffiti from the article?
- Did the article influence your opinion? Explain why or why not.

Check students' answers to be sure they understood the concepts in the article.

Reach All Learners

Build Fluency Choose a section from the article for Paired Reading.

- Have student pairs read the section silently.
- Direct one student to read aloud while the other follows along silently, making notes.
- Once the first student is finished reading, the student who listened acts as coach, providing suggestions and feedback. Students then reverse roles.

Use Small Groups Use an art activity to summarize and extend the theme of the article.

- Have students work in small groups to come up with a slogan to discourage taggers from destroying public property.
- Tell groups to design a poster that will promote their message.
- Have each group present its poster to the class. Discuss the slogans and their effectiveness.

Assist Students Having Difficulty If students struggle to use new words in context, allow them to work with partners.

- Have students complete the Vocabulary Square graphic organizer with partners.
- Provide dictionaries for support. Allow students to look up meanings of new words before writing their own definitions.

WRITING JOURNAL

Extend

Write About It Students will write a letter to the city council.

- Read and discuss the Writing Prompt. (Journal, p. 10) Review the Writing Rubric.
- Encourage students to add more points to the rubric to guide their work.
- Model how to use the organizer.
- Students should use the Check It and Fix It Section and Writing Checklist to revise and evaluate their work.

Model revising by thinking aloud:

> **THINK ALOUD** *As I reread my letter to make sure I have included reasons that support my opinion, I also make sure I have stated my opinion clearly. If there is anything missing, I can add it to my letter as I revise.*

Vocabulary Workshop Students extend their thinking about Word Bank words.

- Students work in pairs or small groups on the Define It organizer. (Journal, p. 12)
- Have students add words to the Your Choice box and their personal word bank.
- Use the Show You Know exercise to assess students' understanding.

Teaching Tip Have students use a dictionary to find other words for the All in the Family exercise. Tell partners to write a sentence for each new word. Ask volunteers to read their sentences to the whole class to check word meanings and correct usage.

UNIT 1

Cross Your Fingers!

PROGRAM RESOURCES

ANTHOLOGY pp. 16–19

TEACHING GUIDE AND RESOURCES
- Guess It and Check It Chart **p. 143**
- Making Personal Connections Organizer **p. 147**
- Answer Key **p. 114**

REAL WORLD WRITING JOURNAL pp. 14–17

ANTHOLOGY

Preteach

Activate Prior Knowledge Draw the Real-Life Connection chart on the board and ask students to provide examples of superstitions. Students will revisit answers after they read.

Build Background *Each leaf of the four-leaf clover is said to represent a quality people would like to have*—faith, love, hope, *and* luck. *What other positive qualities might a lucky symbol represent?*

Introduce Vocabulary

- Have students work with partners to find each boldface vocabulary word in the article.
- Display or distribute the Guess It and Check It Chart. Have students complete the first three columns of the chart. Then have students check their answers against the definitions in the Word Bank.
- *Build Academic Vocabulary* Write the word *explain* on the board. Have volunteers name other forms of this word, such as *explanation*, *explainable*, and *explanatory* and use these words in sentences.

Teach

Focus on the Big Question Ask the Article BQ, "Is there any truth to superstitions?" Students will answer this question after reading.

- *Connect to the Unit Big Question* Have students read the Unit and Article BQs. Ask volunteers to share similarities they notice between the two questions.

Preread the Article Before students read, model how to preview and predict:

> **THINK ALOUD** *I am going to read the title first, because the title usually tells what an article is about. I see*

> *the title is "Cross Your Fingers." That makes me think the article will be about some of the things superstitious people do to prevent bad luck. I am going to look at the pictures, captions, and subheads to gather more information.*

Model how to preview the other text features mentioned in the Think Aloud above. Then ask students to write a prediction about the article.

Conduct a Guided Reading Read the article to the students as they follow along. Pause after each section to monitor students' comprehension.

- Distribute the Making Personal Connections Organizer.
- Have students fill in the graphic organizer as they read.

Reflect on the Article After reading the article, review ideas introduced before or during reading.

- Review the superstitions chart the class completed before reading. Ask students if they read about any other superstitions they can add to the chart.
- Have students reread their predictions and discuss their accuracy.

Practice and Apply

Discuss the Questions Gauge students' comprehension and help them develop critical reading skills. (Answer Key, p. 114)

Connect to the Big Question Write the Article BQ on the board. Have students consider what is true about superstitions.

- Ask volunteers to give examples of the origins of superstitions mentioned in the article. Have students discuss how they could find out if these stories really happened.
- Have students debate the effectiveness of superstitions. Ask them to consider: Do superstitions really work, or do people's beliefs cause them to work?

Assess

Have students summarize the article in their own words. Remind students that a good summary includes a topic sentence that tells what the article is about. Encourage students to provide details they recall from the article in their summaries.

Reach All Learners

Build Fluency Choose a section from the article and instruct students to read aloud for correct pronunciation.

- Read a paragraph aloud, modeling correct pronunciation.
- Have students select a section and read aloud to a partner.
- Have partners share any words that were mispronounced. Repeat the process so that both students read aloud, focusing on correct pronunciation.

Use Small Groups Have students work in small groups to answer one of the questions in the Use Clues section.

- Organize students into small groups and ask them to carefully read question five.
- Groups can devise a "test" of a supersition. How would they set up the experiment? How would they measure the results?
- If time allows, students can test their experiments and report the results to the class. This small group work will also prepare them for the Writing Journal assignment.

Assist Students Having Difficulty If students struggle to summarize the article, have them work with partners.

- Have students tell partners what the article was about.
- Direct partners to take notes on what they hear. Then have students write the summary based on their notes.

WRITING JOURNAL

Extend

Write About It Students will write an experiment to test a superstition.

- Read and discuss the Writing Prompt. (Journal, p. 14) Review the Writing Rubric.
- Encourage students to add more points to the rubric to guide their work.
- Model how to use the organizer.
- Students should use the Check It and Fix It Section and Writing Checklist to revise and evaluate their work.

Model how to organize by thinking aloud:

> **THINK ALOUD** *I want to make sure I select a superstition I can test. I can test a superstition that involves an object, such as a lucky rubber band. How can I test my superstition? I will think of an experiment and write the steps in order. Words like* first, next, *and* last *help organize my thoughts.*

Vocabulary Workshop Students extend their thinking about Word Bank words.

- Students work in pairs or small groups on the Define It organizer. (Journal, p. 16)
- Have students add words to the Your Choice box and their personal word bank.
- Use the Show You Know exercise to assess students' understanding.

Teaching Tip After partners have checked the Show You Know answers, ask volunteers to share their responses with the class. Take an informal poll to see how many students had similar ideas.

The Word on Bullies

PROGRAM RESOURCES

ANTHOLOGY pp. 20–23

TEACHING GUIDE AND RESOURCES
- Two-Column Journal **p. 153**
- Answer Key **p. 114**

REAL WORLD WRITING JOURNAL pp. 18–21

ANTHOLOGY

Preteach

Activate Prior Knowledge Read aloud the Real-Life Connection. Have students copy and complete the chart. Students will revisit answers after they read.

Build Background *Bullying is when someone does or says something that creates power over another person. Bullying can involve physical threats, name-calling, or ignoring someone. Over 5.7 million students in the United States are involved in bullying—either as a participant, a target, or both. In 2005, 28 percent of students reported having been bullied at school.*

Introduce Vocabulary

- Read aloud the sentences from the article in which boldface vocabulary words appear. Discuss what each word means in context.
- Give students the opportunity to practice the vocabulary words in a new context. Work with students to create new sentences for each word.
- *Build Academic Vocabulary* Have students read the academic vocabulary words aloud. Ask volunteers how they might use these words in other classes.

Teach

Focus on the Big Question Ask the Article BQ, "What is the truth about bullies?" Students will answer this question after reading.

- *Connect to the Unit Big Question* Write the Unit and Article BQs on the board. With students, circle similar words and ideas to show how the BQs are linked.

Preread the Article Before students read, model how to preview and predict:

THINK ALOUD *I am going to preview the article by reading the introduction. The introduction to the article appears above the title. The title of this article is "The Word on Bullies." I can use the introduction and the title to make a prediction about what the article will be about. I think this article will be about why bullies pick on other kids.*

Model how to preview the first paragraph of the article. Then ask students to write a prediction about the article.

Conduct a Guided Reading Read the article to the students as they follow along. Pause after each section to monitor students' comprehension.

- Ask "5 Ws and an H" questions.
- Have volunteers summarize the strategies for handling a bully.

Reflect on the Article After reading the article, review ideas introduced before or during reading.

- Have students reread their charts from the Real-Life Connection. Tell them to add ideas they learned from the article.
- Ask students if they would change their predictions after reading. Have them explain why.

Practice and Apply

Discuss the Questions Gauge students' comprehension and help them develop critical reading skills. (Answer Key, p. 114)

Connect to the Big Question Use the Two-Column Journal to have students answer the question.

- Have students write the Article BQ on their organizers and write details from the article that answer the question in the first column.
- Then have students list their own ideas in the "My Thoughts" column.

Assess

Have students role-play a situation involving a bully. Tell students to try one of the strategies presented in the article in their role play. Give students time to practice and then ask volunteers to present their scenes to the class. Conclude with a discussion about which strategies might be more effective than others.

Reach All Learners

Build Fluency Choose a section from the article to practice fluency.

- Model reading aloud with expression.
- Have students choral read the section, focusing on reading with expression.
- Ask volunteers to read other sections of the text for the whole class. Check to see that students are reading with expression.

Use Small Groups Have students review or consider how a school's bullying policy can help students.

- Distribute copies of your school's bullying policy to students. Have students work in small groups to review the school rules about bullying.
- Have students compare and contrast the school policy with ideas and strategies presented in the article.
- If no school policy is available, have students create a proposal for a school policy.

Assist Students Having Difficulty If students struggle to make connections between the BQs, provide them with a two-column chart to compare and contrast.

- Remind students that when we compare, we look at similarities. When we contrast, we look at differences.
- Have students tell a partner what they think is similar and different between the two BQs.

WRITING JOURNAL

Extend

Write About It Students will write a letter of advice for the school newspaper.

- Read and discuss the Writing Prompt. (Journal, p. 18) Review the Writing Rubric.
- Encourage students to add more points to the rubric to guide their work.
- Model how to use the organizer.
- Students should use the Check It and Fix It Section and Writing Checklist to revise and evaluate their work.

Model drafting by thinking aloud:

> **THINK ALOUD** *I want to be sure that I write about the strategy I think is best for dealing with a bully. I can look back to the strategies I took notes on to decide which one to include in my letter. As I draft, I put those strategies in my words, not the author's. The letter needs to have my "voice." It should sound like me.*

Vocabulary Workshop Students extend their thinking about Word Bank words.

- Students work in pairs or small groups on the Define It organizer. (Journal, p. 20)
- Have students add words to the Your Choice box and their personal word bank.
- Use the Show You Know exercise to assess students' understanding.

Teaching Tip Have students read the dialogues they wrote for Show You Know with a partner. Tell students to discuss how they used the new words in their dialogues. Ask volunteers to present their conversations to the whole class.

Campers Give Peace a Chance

PROGRAM RESOURCES

ANTHOLOGY pp. 24–27

TEACHING GUIDE AND RESOURCES
- Word Pyramid **p. 157**
- Opinion and Reasons Organizer **p. 148**
- Answer Key **p. 115**

REAL WORLD WRITING JOURNAL pp. 22–25

ANTHOLOGY

Preteach

Activate Prior Knowledge Have students copy and complete the chart in the Real-Life Connection. Ask volunteers to tell what they know about peace camps.

Build Background *Kids from Israel and Palestine may live very close to each other in their home countries, yet never meet. When these kids attend peace camps in the United States, they meet for the first time and get the chance to know each other.*

Introduce Vocabulary

- Draw or display the Word Pyramid. Have students choose two words from the word bank for this activity.
- Have students write the word, an antonym, and a sentence using each vocabulary word on their Word Pyramid.
- *Build Academic Vocabulary* Review academic vocabulary with students. Have students *debate* a current event topic in which they are trying to *convince* other groups that they have better *insight* about the topic.

Teach

Focus on the Big Question Ask the Article BQ, "What is the best way to understand people who are different?" Students will answer this question after reading.

- *Connect to the Unit Big Question* Have students read the Unit BQ and Article BQ with a partner. Ask students whether they think there is just one or more than one true answer to the Article BQ.

Preread the Article Before students read, model how to preview the title and subtitles:

THINK ALOUD *The title of this article is "Campers Give Peace a Chance." The subtitles are in bold at the top of each section. "Enemies Become Friends" and "The Key to Understanding" are the subtitles. I predict this article is about a camp that brings people together.*

Ask students to write predictions to revisit after reading.

Conduct a Guided Reading Read the article to the students as they follow along. Pause after each section to monitor students' comprehension.

- Have students ask a question after reading each section.
- Ask students to identify the countries on the map on p. 25.

Reflect on the Article After reading the article, review ideas introduced before or during reading.

- Have students revisit the Real-Life Connection chart and discuss what they learned about peace camps from the article.
- Ask students if they would change their predictions. Have them explain why.

Practice and Apply

Discuss the Questions Gauge students' comprehension and help them develop critical reading skills. (Answer Key, p. 115)

Connect to the Big Question Use the Opinion and Reasons organizer to have students answer the Article BQ.

- Tell students to write their opinions about how to understand people who are different.
- Tell students to write reasons that support their opinions based on the article.

Assess

Have students imagine that they are camp counselors at a peace camp. Tell students to design a game or think of an existing game that would support the goals of the peace camp. Then tell them to explain how the game supports the kind of learning described in the article. Have students answer the question: How does this game teach respect and understanding for others?

Reach All Learners

Build Fluency Choose a section from the article for an Echo Reading.

- Tell students to pause at appropriate punctuation as they read aloud.
- Have students read a section aloud to a partner, pausing at appropriate punctuation. Students then reverse roles.
- Have students revisit the paragraph they read aloud, pointing out the punctuation that indicates a reader should pause.

Use Small Groups Use a discussion activity to encourage students to make connections between text and self.

- Have students share experiences they have had at camp or with teams or clubs.
- Tell students to make comparisons between their camp experience and the peace camps described in the article.
- Have students conclude by listing what they learned at camp. Ask students to discuss what kids learn at camp that complements what they learn in school.

Assist Students Having Difficulty If students struggle to identify antonyms for Word Bank words, provide them with a dictionary or thesaurus.

- Review the difference between antonyms and synonyms.
- Have students practice using a reference book, looking up antonyms for each word.

WRITING JOURNAL

Extend

Write About It Students will create a brochure for a peace camp.

- Read and discuss the Writing Prompt. (Journal, p. 22) Review the Writing Rubric.
- Encourage students to add more points to the rubric to guide their work.
- Model how to use the organizer.
- Students should use the Check It and Fix It Section and Writing Checklist to revise and evaluate their work.

Model revising by thinking aloud:

> **THINK ALOUD** *I will read over my writing to make sure I have included everything and my words make sense. Reading aloud is a good way to check my work. If I stumble over words or sentences, I can double-check them to make sure I used the correct words and punctuation.*

Vocabulary Workshop Students extend their thinking about Word Bank words.

- Students work in pairs or small groups on the graphic organizer. (Journal, p. 24)
- Have students add words to the Your Choice box and their personal word bank.
- Use the Show You Know exercise to assess students' understanding.

Teaching Tip After students complete the Word Endings activity, ask volunteers to read their sentences aloud to the class. Then have students suggest other common words that end in *-ion*, *-tion*, and *-ation*, such as *education*, and list the words on the board.

PROGRAM RESOURCES

ANTHOLOGY pp. 28–31

TEACHING GUIDE AND RESOURCES
- T-Chart **p. 151**
- Series of Events Map **p. 150**
- Answer Key **p. 115**

REAL WORLD WRITING JOURNAL pp. 26–29

ANTHOLOGY

Preteach

Activate Prior Knowledge Have students work in small groups to discuss the questions in the Real-Life Connection. Ask each group to share its ideas with the class. Students will revisit answers after they read.

Build Background *Sierra Leone is a country in West Africa. Ishmael Beah was a boy living in Sierra Leone when war broke out in his country. Civil wars in Africa and other countries sometimes force children to become soldiers. Human rights groups estimate that there are 300,000 child soldiers worldwide.*

Introduce Vocabulary

- Have students read the words and definitions in the Word Bank. Ask volunteers to identify a synonym for each word.
- Display or distribute the T-Chart. Tell students to choose two words from the Word Bank and list synonyms for each word.
- *Build Academic Vocabulary* Create a word web for one academic vocabulary word on the board and have students make connections to other words they know.

Teach

Focus on the Big Question Ask the Article BQ, "How do events in our lives shape the truth of who we are?" Students will answer this question after reading.

- *Connect to the Unit Big Question* Have students reread the Unit BQ. Discuss with students some truths about their own lives. Ask volunteers to list ways to learn the truth about someone.

Preread the Article Before students read, model how to preview topic sentences and make predictions about content:

> **THINK ALOUD** *I am going to skim the article to make a prediction about what it is about. I can read topic sentences when I preview an article for information. Topic sentences usually contain the main idea for each paragraph. Let's read the topic sentences together.*

Model reading topic sentences to preview the article. Then ask students to write a prediction.

Conduct a Guided Reading Read the article to the students as they follow along. Pause after each section to monitor students' comprehension.

- Have students make connections between the text and the world as they read.
- Ask students to make an inference about the effects of war on children.

Reflect on the Article After reading the article, review ideas introduced before or during reading.

- Revisit the questions from the Real-Life Connection. Have students discuss answers they learned from the article.
- Have students reread their predictions and discuss their accuracy.

Practice and Apply

Discuss the Questions Gauge students' comprehension and help them develop critical reading skills. (Answer Key, p. 115)

Connect to the Big Question Refocus students' attention on the Article BQ. Use the Series of Events Map to have students answer the question.

- Have students write the Article BQ on their organizers. Tell them to refer back to the article and list the events of Ishmael Beah's life in the order they occurred.
- Call for volunteers to answer the BQ. Students should support their ideas with events from the article. Have students refer to their graphic organizers for support.

Assess

Have students create a Learning Log and answer these three questions:

- How do the dangers kids in the United States encounter compare to dangers in war-torn countries?
- How do you feel about what you have read?
- List three resources where you could find more information on this topic.

Reach All Learners

Build Fluency Choose a section from the article for a Paired Reading.

- Have student pairs read the section silently.
- Direct one student to read the section aloud while the other takes notes.
- Once the first student is finished reading, the student who listened acts as coach, providing suggestions and feedback. Students then reverse roles.

Use Small Groups Use a Write-Around activity for the third Use Clues question.

- In groups of four, have each student begin with a piece of paper with the Article BQ written across the top.
- Have students write a response for one minute and then pass their papers to the right. The one-minute writing begins again, and students add to the paper in front of them.
- Continue until all four students have written on each paper. Share writing in a class discussion.

Assist Students Having Difficulty If students struggle to list events in the correct sequence, suggest signal words that can help them order their ideas.

- Have students list the events from the article.
- Then tell students to read the events to a partner, using signal words such as *first, second, then, next,* and *finally* to put events in the correct order.

WRITING JOURNAL

Extend

Write About It Students will write an introductory speech.

- Read and discuss the Writing Prompt. (Journal, p. 26) Review the Writing Rubric.
- Encourage students to add more points to the rubric to guide their work.
- Model how to use the organizer.
- Students should use the Check It and Fix It Section and Writing Checklist to revise and evaluate their work.

Model organizing ideas in a speech by thinking aloud:

THINK ALOUD *I want to be sure that I include the important details from Ishmael Beah's life. First I will write the details I remember. What order makes the most sense? I will put them in the order of Beah's life. That will make sense to listeners.*

Vocabulary Workshop Students extend their thinking about Word Bank words.

- Students work in pairs or small groups on the Define It organizer. (Journal, p. 28)
- Have students add words to the Your Choice box and their personal word bank.
- Use the Show You Know exercise to assess students' understanding.

Teaching Tip Have students circle the Word Bank word they could use in conversation at home or at school. Tell students to use the word at least once in school today. You can create a game by awarding students points for both using the words and catching someone using Word Bank words in conversation.

UNIT 1

Luol Deng: A True Winner

PROGRAM RESOURCES

ANTHOLOGY pp. 32–35

TEACHING GUIDE AND RESOURCES
- Cause and Effect Map **p. 140**
- Answer Key **p. 115**

REAL WORLD WRITING JOURNAL pp. 30–33

ANTHOLOGY

Preteach

Activate Prior Knowledge Have students write a response to the questions in the Real-Life Connection. Students will revisit answers after they read.

Build Background *When it becomes too dangerous for people to stay in their own country, they may seek refuge at refugee camps. These camps are thought of as temporary, but when wars go on for decades, generations can end up living in refugee camps. At some camps, there is no fresh water, electricity, or adequate health care. Diseases can spread quickly.*

Introduce Vocabulary

- Have students scan the article to find the sentences with boldface vocabulary words. Ask volunteers to read these sentences aloud.
- Pairs write a definition for each word. Have students compare their definitions with those in the Word Bank.
- *Build Academic Vocabulary* Work with students to identify academic vocabulary words. Ask volunteers how they might use these words in their daily lives.

Teach

Focus on the Big Question Ask the Article BQ, "How has Deng's past made him the true winner he is today?" Students will answer this question after reading.

- *Connect to the Unit Big Question* Read the Unit and Article BQs aloud. Ask volunteers to share what similarities they notice in the questions.

Preread the Article Before students read, model how to preview graphic features:

THINK ALOUD *Articles sometimes use graphic features to give information that supports the text. This article has a photo and a map. I can use these graphic features to make a prediction about the article. The photo shows a basketball player. The map shows the continent of Africa. I think this article will be about a basketball player from Africa.*

Model writing a prediction based on graphic features. Then ask students to write a prediction.

Conduct a Guided Reading Read the article to the students as they follow along. Pause after each section to monitor students' comprehension.

- Have students pause to ask questions as they read.
- Call on a volunteer to summarize the section.

Reflect on the Article After reading the article, review ideas introduced before or during reading.

- Have students reread their responses to the Real-Life Connection. Ask them why people look up to Deng for his heart.
- Have students discuss changes they could make to their predictions.

Practice and Apply

Discuss the Questions Gauge students' comprehension and help them develop critical reading skills. (Answer Key, p. 115)

Connect to the Big Question Use the Cause and Effect Map to have students answer the Article BQ.

- Have students write the Article BQ on their organizers. Model writing the cause in the main circle: Deng remembers his homeland and the people of Sudan.
- Tell students to write three effects on the Map. How do these effects make Deng a "true winner"?

Assess

Have students work with partners to write questions they would like to ask Luol Deng. Tell students to imagine they could interview Deng about his homeland and his work today. Have students write five questions and then role-play an interview, answering the questions based on the information in the article.

Reach All Learners

Build Fluency Choose a section from the article for an Echo Reading.

- Model reading aloud with correct pronunciation and phrasing.
- Have volunteers echo read the same section. Ask students to self-assess their pronunciation and phrasing.
- Have students work with a partner to select another section for an echo read. Tell partners to take turns reading the section aloud, practicing correct pronunciation and phrasing.

Use Small Groups Have students research and write a presentation on the Sudan region today.

- Have groups read recent newspapers and magazines to learn more about the Sudan.
- Tell students to take notes on the people of the Sudan and their lives. Have each group include information on refugees and their living conditions.
- Each group should use their notes for a three-minute oral presentation on the Sudan.

Assist Students Having Difficulty If students struggle to write questions for the assessment activity, provide them with an outline for asking questions.

- The outline should include the "5 Ws and an H" questions.
- Ask the whole class for examples of possible questions before students begin writing independently.

WRITING JOURNAL

Extend

Write About It Students will write a note describing a mosquito net.

- Read and discuss the Writing Prompt. (Journal, p. 30) Review the Writing Rubric.
- Encourage students to add more points to the rubric to guide their work.
- Model how to use the organizer.
- Students should use the Check It and Fix It Section and Writing Checklist to revise and evaluate their work.

Model drafting by thinking aloud:

> **THINK ALOUD** *I want to be sure that I explain everything I need to explain about mosquito nets. I will think about the questions* who, what, why, *and* how *as I write my note. These questions will guide my ideas. When I have answered each question, my note will be complete.*

Vocabulary Workshop Students extend their thinking about Word Bank words.

- Students work in pairs or small groups on the Define It organizer. (Journal, p. 32)
- Have students add words to the Your Choice box and their personal word bank.
- Use the Show You Know exercise to assess students' understanding.

Teaching Tip After students have reviewed their Show You Know answers with partners, have them discuss how they used background knowledge as well as an understanding of word meanings to write each explanation.

PROGRAM RESOURCES

ANTHOLOGY
Unit 1 Closer pp. 36–37

What is the best way to find the truth?

Introduce the Unit Project

Interview Students will participate in an interview, discussing and presenting an answer to the Big Question: *What is the best way to find the truth?*

- Read through the steps of the assignment with students.
- Point out the rubric so that students will know their goals for the assignment. Add other rubric points with students to guide their work.
- Allow time for students to practice and present their work. Encourage listeners to offer their feedback and advice on the presentation.

Model Model how to plan a complete response by thinking aloud:

> **THINK ALOUD** *As I plan my response, I want to make sure I have good reasons that support my ideas. I will include details from the articles that helped me decide the best way to find the truth. I will also include a real-life example about a time I had to decide what was true for me. Supporting my answer with details from the articles and my own example completes my interview notes.*

Teaching Tip Remind students that their real-life examples should explain how they decided what was true for them. Monitor students to make sure they don't get sidetracked describing a problem.

Conclude the Unit

Review Unit Objectives Return to the unit objectives and ask students to evaluate how well they mastered each one on a scale of 1 to 5, with 1 being low and 5 being high. Discuss how lower scores could be improved.

Reflect on the Learning Examine the unit collage with students. Ask them to reflect on what they have learned. They can write or discuss with the class or in small groups. Prompt students' thinking with questions such as:

- What was the most interesting article you read? What did you like about it?
- How did your ideas about truth change as you read the articles?
- Which topic would you like to know more about? What do you still wonder about it?
- How did the writing assignments and the interview help you form your ideas about the best way to find the truth?
- How could you use what you learned during this unit?

Name _____

Word Bank Quiz

WORD LIST A			
affect	convince	explain	observe
awareness	debate	factual	reality
consequence	evidence	mean	reveal

Ten of the unit Word Bank words are defined in parentheses in the article below. As you read the article, use Word List A, above, to figure out which word best fits each definition. Write the word on the line provided. (You will not use every word on the list.) Then go on to the next page of the quiz.

Debating the Truth about Global Warming

Are temperatures on Earth rising as one **(1. result)** _____ of carbon dioxide in the atmosphere? Scientists collect facts that may **(2. show something that was hidden)** _____ the cause of global warming. But many people disagree about the causes of rising temperatures. People often **(3. give reasons for or against)** _____ the topic of global warming.

Some say that there is not enough **(4. something that shows it is true)** _____ of global warming. They believe global warming is not **(5. real)** _____. Those who doubt the **(6. things that exist in the real world)** _____ of global warming say that temperature changes do not mean the environment is threatened. They **(7. give reasons)** _____ rising temperatures as a natural event.

However, many believe that carbon dioxide does **(8. create a change)** _____ the environment and cause temperature changes.

Environmentalists work to educate people and raise **(9. knowing about a problem)** _____. They try to **(10. make people feel sure)** _____ people that everyone should help reduce carbon dioxide in the atmosphere.

WORD LIST B			
believable	fiction	observe	rarely
conclude	insight	pattern	report
evaluate	mean	perceive	view

Ten more Word Bank words are defined in parentheses in the story below. As you read the story, use Word List B, above, to figure out which word best fits each definition. Write the word on the line provided. (You will not use every word on the list.)

Discovering the Truth

One evening last week I found myself right in the middle of a mystery. I returned home from basketball practice to an empty house. This **(11. does not happen often)** _____ happens. Usually my mother and sister are home in the evening. I could only **(12. figure out)** _____ that my family had vanished. Or had they really vanished? I decided to **(13. to form an opinion of)** _____ the facts. The house was empty. That much was easy for me to **(14. notice)** _____. Was a disappearance the most **(15. possible or true)** _____ cause, though? I decided to do further research.

I walked from room to room. It took me a while to **(16. watch carefully)** _____ all the rooms of the house. However, I did not discover any **(17. a way that does not change)** _____ of clues. This does not **(18. to show or give a sign)** _____ I gave up the search. I held on to a hopeful **(19. opinion)** _____ of the possibilities. My optimism was rewarded when I realized my dog Jasper was not in the house either!

The missing dog gave me a new **(20. clear understanding)** _____ about what was really going on: a dog walk. The truth behind the case of the vanishing family brought a smile to my face. I had solved the mystery.

 # Does every conflict have a winner?

Unit Overview

The articles in this unit explore the topic of conflict. As students read about conflicts that occur between individuals, between groups, and within individuals, they will decide for themselves whether or not every conflict has a winner.

Launch the Unit

Connect to the Big Question Prompt students' thinking about the unit opener. Read the introduction with students and examine the illustration. Ask questions such as:

- *What are some different kinds of conflict people can have?*
- *Describe the conflict in the illustration.*
- *Do you think the students in the picture might feel a conflict inside themselves? What would it be?*
- *In this case, does a tie mean there is no winner? Thinking about this situation, how would you answer the Big Question?*
- *What connections do you have to this situation?*

Use the prompt on the page as the basis for journal writing or for small group or whole class discussion. Students can share their ideas with partners or in small groups.

Anchor Students' Thinking Start a bulletin board on which you post the Big Question. Throughout the unit, students can add to the bulletin board. Use ideas such as the following:

- Ask students what conflicts are described in the articles and whether those conflicts have clear winners. Students can post their ideas.
- Have students look through the articles and other sources for words that can be used to talk about conflict. Students can post these words and their meanings.
- Place exemplary writing from students' writing journal assignments on the bulletin board. Discuss with students what these writings reveal about conflict.
- Encourage students to add other examples of conflict, such as newspaper or magazine articles, photographs culled from print or online resources, and so on. Link students' findings to ideas in the articles and to the Unit Big Question.

Unit Objectives

Share these objectives with students. As you read the articles in this unit, you will:

- Identify different types of conflicts and their results.
- Determine an answer to the Big Question: *Does every conflict have a winner?* Explain your answer using details from the articles and from your own experiences.
- Use vocabulary words to talk and write about conflict.
- Form an opinion for a debate and support that opinion with facts.

Athletes as Role Models

PROGRAM RESOURCES

ANTHOLOGY pp. 40–43

TEACHING GUIDE AND RESOURCES
- Venn Diagram **p. 154**
- Three-Column Chart **p. 152**
- Answer Key **p. 117**

REAL WORLD WRITING JOURNAL pp. 36–39

ANTHOLOGY

Preteach

Activate Prior Knowledge Ask students to name some famous athletes. Write the names on the board. Then have students fill out the Venn Diagram with the athletes' names.

Build Background *The Democratic Republic of the Congo (DRC) is also called Congo-Kinshasa. There is also another country in Africa with the name Congo. That country is the Republic of the Congo, or Congo-Brazzaville. Brazzaville and Kinshasa are the capitals of the different countries.*

Introduce Vocabulary

- Read aloud the definition of each word and the example sentences.
- Have student pairs find the boldface vocabulary words in the selection. Ask students to take turns reading aloud the sentences and discuss word meanings.
- *Build Academic Vocabulary* Ask volunteers to locate words in the Word Bank that relate to conflict. Point out the words *disagreement* and *understanding*. Discuss with students how to move from a *disagreement* to an *understanding*.

Teach

Focus on the Big Question Ask the Article BQ, "Should athletes be role models who help others 'win'?" Students will answer this question after reading.

- *Connect to the Unit Big Question* Write the Unit and Article BQs on the board. Discuss with students the meaning of the term *conflict*.

Preread the Article Before students read, model how to preview and predict:

THINK ALOUD *I see the title is "Athletes as Role Models." That tells me that the article is about how athletes act. I see the boldface words* model *and* scandal. *That makes me think that the article will show one athlete who is a role model and another who is not.*

Model how to preview pictures and captions. Then have students write a prediction.

Conduct a Guided Reading Read the article to students as they follow along. Pause after each section to monitor students' comprehension.

- After the first section discuss whether Dikembe Mutombo is a good role model.
- After the second section discuss whether Sammy Sosa is a good role model.
- After the third section discuss whether the class agrees with Charles Barkley.

Reflect on the Article After reading the article, review ideas introduced before or during reading.

- Have students look at their Venn Diagrams. Would they change their diagrams? Have students explain why.
- Ask students to revisit their predictions about the article. Were their predictions correct?

Practice and Apply

Discuss the Questions Gauge students' comprehension and help them develop critical reading skills. (Answer Key, p. 117)

Connect to the Big Question Use the Three-Column Chart to have students focus on the BQ.

- Draw the graphic organizer on the board.
- Label the second and third columns *Example* and *Argument*. Label rows: *Good Role Model, Bad Role Model, Both or Neither*.
- Model how to fill out the first row. Have students complete the organizer.

Assess

Use this informal assessment before moving on to the Writing Journal activities. Have students write one or two sentences about their favorite sports (or entertainment) star and whether that athlete is a good role model. Read through their writing to gauge students' understanding of the concept of "role model."

Reach All Learners

Build Fluency Choose a section from the article and read aloud to students.

- Model fluent reading of a section. Use as much expression as possible.
- Have students follow along silently.
- Have students echo your reading, copying your expression.

Use Small Groups Use a discussion activity to engage students in active learning.

- Arrange students in groups of four. Have each group come up with a written answer to the BQ. The answer should also explain why the group came to that conclusion.
- Have students use their Example/Argument charts to discuss the BQ.
- When each group has completed its discussion, groups can share conclusions with the class.

Assist Students Having Difficulty If students struggle to answer the first Use Clues question, ask the following questions:

- What does corking do to a bat? (It makes it lighter. It makes it easier to swing.)
- What effect do corked bats have on how far the ball goes? (Corked bats make the ball go farther.)
- Is it fair for some players to use corked bats if other players do not use corked bats?

WRITING JOURNAL

Extend

Write About It Students will write a speech about Dikembe Mutombo.

- Read and discuss the Writing Prompt. (Journal, p. 36) Review the Writing Rubric. Encourage students to add more points to the rubric to guide their work.
- Model how to use the organizer.
- Students should use the Check It and Fix It Section and Writing Checklist to revise and evaluate their work.

Model drafting by thinking aloud:

> **THINK ALOUD** *As I draft, I add details about Dikembe Mutombo that answer the questions who and why. The "who" is Dikembe Mutombo. The "why" is that he is a good person. That is not enough information for the speech. Plus, it is not very interesting. I will add details about him to keep the audience interested and to tell more about my main points.*

As you think aloud, write notes on the board for students to copy.

Vocabulary Workshop Students extend their thinking about Word Bank words.

- Students work in pairs or small groups on the Define It organizer. (Journal, p. 38)
- Have students add words to the Your Choice box and their personal word bank.
- Use the Show You Know exercise to assess students' understanding.

Teaching Tip After teaching the Word Beginning exercises, have the class brainstorm other words that begin with *dis-*. Write the list on the board. Discuss how the prefix changes word meaning.

UNIT 2

Coyotes on the Go

PROGRAM RESOURCES

ANTHOLOGY pp. 44–47

TEACHING GUIDE AND RESOURCES
• Cause and Effect Map p. 140
• Answer Key p. 117

REAL WORLD WRITING JOURNAL pp. 40–43

ANTHOLOGY

Preteach

Activate Prior Knowledge Help students fill out the rating chart in the Real-Life Connection. Encourage students to share their knowledge. Do a think aloud:

> **THINK ALOUD** *I do not know much about coyotes, but I do remember the Road Runner cartoon. That cartoon took place in the desert. I wonder if all coyotes live in the desert?*

Build Background *Coyotes can run almost 40 miles per hour and can climb over a five-foot fence. They can travel several hundred miles in one night. Coyotes communicate with one another through a series of woofs, growls, and barks. These sounds tell others of threats that are near and far. They also whine to greet one another and howl to let others know that they have found food.*

Introduce Vocabulary

• Have pairs find the Word Bank words in the article and read the sentences aloud to each other.
• Each pair works together to write questions using all of the Word Bank words. Students will revisit questions after reading.
• *Build Academic Vocabulary* Point out academic vocabulary. *Outcome*, for example, is used in science. Have students create sentences to link academic words to different subject areas.

Teach

Focus on the Big Question Ask the Article BQ, "Does anyone win when people and wild animals come into conflict?" Students will answer this question after reading.

• *Connect to the Unit Big Question* Write the Unit and Article BQs on the board. Ask students if they can think of an example of humans and wild animals that live in the same area and do not get into conflict.

Preread the Article Help students prepare to read the article by looking at and reading the title, illustrations, and graphics.

• Have students identify any words in the title and graphics they don't understand. Explain meanings.
• Have students set a purpose for reading.

Conduct a Guided Reading Read the article to students as they follow along. Pause after each section to monitor students' comprehension.

• Ask "5 Ws and an H" questions.
• Ask a volunteer to summarize the section.

Reflect on the Article After reading the article, review ideas introduced before or during reading.

• Have students look at the chart from the Real-Life Connection. Has their knowledge changed?
• Have students answer the questions they wrote earlier using words from the Word Bank.

Practice and Apply

Discuss the Questions Gauge students' comprehension and help them develop critical reading skills. (Answer Key, p. 117)

Connect to the Big Question Have students use the Cause and Effect Map to focus on the BQ.

• Have students work in pairs or small groups.
• Direct students to list in their graphic organizers the causes and effects of humans coming in contact with coyotes.
• Have students answer the BQ using the information in their charts.

Assess

As a group, discuss with students how they feel about coyotes.

- Are they dangerous or not?
- How should cities and towns deal with coyotes?
- Should states create safe places for coyotes?

Assess knowledge as students respond.

Reach All Learners

Build Fluency Choose a section from the article and do a Choral Reading to practice fluency.

- Have students follow along in their books as you read the section aloud.
- Reread the section aloud and have students choral read it with you.
- Then have students choral read the section without you. Stop and correct any pronunciation or fluency errors.

Use Small Groups Place students in small groups to discuss the BQ.

- In groups of three, have students role play. Each group will have one student who speaks for humans, one student who speaks for coyotes, and one student who speaks for squirrels.
- Tell students that they have to represent the point of view of their character in a discussion about the BQ.
- Have each group work out a way to live together and resolve their conflicts.

Assist Students Having Difficulty If students are having difficulty understanding the points in the article, have them answer *who, what, when, where, why,* and *how.*

- Who or what is the article about?
- Where do the events in the article happen?
- When do these events happen? Why?
- How can some of the conflicts be solved?

WRITING JOURNAL

Extend

Write About It Students will write a letter to the editor of a local paper.

- Read and discuss the Writing Prompt. (Journal, p. 40) Review the Writing Rubric. Encourage students to add more points to the rubric to guide their work.
- Model how to use the organizer.
- Students should use the Check It and Fix It Section and Writing Checklist to revise and evaluate their work.

Teaching Tip Discuss with the class what would be the best order to list their reasons. Should the most powerful reason go first or last? Remind students that they are trying to persuade people who are reading the letter. They want to leave a strong impression.

Vocabulary Workshop Students extend their thinking about Word Bank words.

- Students work in pairs or small groups on the Define It organizer. (Journal, p. 42)
- Have students fill out the Your Choice box and their personal word bank.
- Use the Show You Know exercise to assess students' understanding.

As you write definitions, model by thinking aloud:

THINK ALOUD *The word* enact *has two parts. The prefix* en- *means "to cause." The word* act *means "to do something." So* enact *means "to cause something to happen."*

Moms and Dads in the Military

PROGRAM RESOURCES

ANTHOLOGY pp. 48–51

TEACHING GUIDE AND RESOURCES
- Guess It and Check It Chart **p. 143**
- T-Chart **p. 151**
- Answer Key **p. 117**

REAL WORLD WRITING JOURNAL pp. 44–47

ANTHOLOGY

Preteach

Activate Prior Knowledge Take a poll of "agree" or "disagree" for each question in the Real-Life Connection. Students will revisit answers after they read.

Build Background *Since September 11, 2001, more than 90,000 American women have served as fighter pilots, medics, military police, and other positions in the global war on terror.*

Introduce Vocabulary

- Read aloud the sentences from the article in which boldface vocabulary words appear.
- Have students fill out the first three boxes in the Guess It and Check It Chart. Model how to guess:

> **THINK ALOUD** *The first paragraph says a young military couple faced a problem they did not "plan" for. One clue I see is the phrase "they had to think about." My guess is that* plan *means "I get ready for."*

- *Build Academic Vocabulary* Ask volunteers to locate words in the Word Bank that might be used when discussing a solution to a conflict. For example, *plan* and *resolution* can be used to discuss possible solutions to conflict.

Teach

Focus on the Big Question Ask the Article BQ, "Do we need new laws to protect mothers and fathers in the military?" Students will answer this question after reading.

- *Connect to the Unit Big Question* Ask students how *conflict* is connected to the Article BQ. Discuss with students why this issue might

cause a conflict among people who have different opinions.

Preread the Article Before students read, take another poll of the class.

- Ask students if they have any family members who are in or have ever been in the military. Tally their responses on the board.
- What do they know about military life for families?
- Tell students that bringing their own experiences to reading helps them better understand what they read.

Conduct a Guided Reading Read the article to the students as they follow along. Pause after each section to monitor students' comprehension.

- *What does the author mean with the words "if neither of them returned from war"?*
- *What does* serve *mean in the article?*
- *What situation does the military face today?*

Reflect on the Article After reading the article, review ideas introduced before or during reading.

- Retake the poll from the Real-Life Connection. Have answers changed? Ask students why.
- Tell students that good readers often finish reading with new questions. Ask students to write something they still wonder about.

Practice and Apply

Discuss the Questions Gauge students' comprehension and help them develop critical reading skills. (Answer Key, p. 117)

Connect to the Big Question Have students use the T-Chart to focus on the BQ.

- Have students write the Article BQ on their organizers. Have them label the columns *Pro* and *Con*.
- Brainstorm with students opinions both for and against changing the laws of the military.

Assess

Use this informal assessment before moving on to the Writing Journal activities.

- What was today's article about?
- What did you already know that was in the article?
- What did you learn that you did not know?
- What was the conflict in the article?

Review students' answers to assess understanding.

Reach All Learners

Build Fluency Choose a section from the article. Read it aloud as students follow along silently.

- Point out to students some of what you did when you read the section. For example, point out when and why you paused (e.g., at commas and periods). Point out reading smoothly through line breaks.
- Read the section aloud again as students read aloud with you.

Use Small Groups Use small groups to help students complete the Find It on the Page questions.

- Place students in small groups. Have each group find and read together the section of the article on the Sullivan brothers.
- Have students work together and use sticky notes to mark where they find the answers to the questions.

Assist Students Having Difficulty If students struggle to understand longer sentences, teach them how to turn long complex sentences into shorter, more understandable chunks.

- Point out a compound or complex sentence in the selection. Read it aloud as two sentences. Ask students if they can understand the two sentences. Read it as one sentence. Ask students if they understand the whole sentence.
- Have students find a different compound or complex sentence. Have them repeat the process.

WRITING JOURNAL

Extend

Write About It Students will write a script for a radio show.

- Read and discuss the Writing Prompt. (Journal, p. 44) Review the Writing Rubric. Encourage students to add more points to the rubric to guide their work.
- Model how to use the organizer.
- Students should use the Check It and Fix It Section and Writing Checklist to revise and evaluate their work.

As you draft, model by thinking aloud:

> **THINK ALOUD** *I want to be sure that my argument makes sense, so I am going to use words such as* also *and* in addition *to help the reader understand my argument. I will make sure that my first point gets the reader's attention. I will need to think of some powerful adjectives to do that.*

Vocabulary Workshop Students extend their thinking about Word Bank words.

- Students work in pairs or small groups on the Define It organizer. (Journal, p. 46)
- Have students add words to the Your Choice box and their personal word bank.
- Use the Show You Know exercise to assess students' understanding.

Teaching Tip Institute a class vocabulary word for each week. Write the word on the board and have students add the word to their word bank. Then use the word in a new sentence each day. Challenge students to use the word in different sentences as well.

UNIT 2

Sports Parents

PROGRAM RESOURCES

ANTHOLOGY pp. 52–55

TEACHING GUIDE AND RESOURCES
- K-W-L Chart **p. 145**
- Two-Column Journal **p. 153**
- Answer Key **p. 118**

REAL WORLD WRITING JOURNAL pp. 48–51

ANTHOLOGY

Preteach

Activate Prior Knowledge Have students answer the questions in the Real-Life Connection. Students will revisit answers after they read.

Build Background *Many sports organizations have rules of conduct to control the behavior of parents. These include the U.S. Figure Skating and the American Junior Golf Associations.*

Introduce Vocabulary

- Write the definitions of the vocabulary words on the board.
- Use each vocabulary word in a sentence as you write the word on the board.
- Have students tell you which definition matches the word you just used in a sentence.
- *Build Academic Vocabulary* Ask students what word they see in the word *compromise* (promise). Explain that *com* is the Latin root for "together." Tell students that a compromise is when two parties work together to resolve a conflict. Have students locate the word in the Word Bank that is needed to find a compromise. (*communication*)

Teach

Focus on the Big Question Ask the Article BQ, "What happens when parents put too much pressure on kids to succeed in sports?" Students will answer this question after reading.

- *Connect to the Unit Big Question* Write the Article BQ on the board. Ask students to think about what this BQ has to do with conflict. Encourage volunteers to give examples.

Preread the Article Before students read, introduce them to the K-W-L strategy.

- Brainstorm as a class answers to the "What do I already know?" question.

- Have students think about and answer the "What do I want to know?" question. Model asking a question before reading:

> **THINK ALOUD** *Now that I know that this article is going to be about parents who are involved in their children's sports activities, I have a question. What might parents do at a sporting event that would be considered bad?*

Conduct a Guided Reading Read the article to the students as they follow along. Pause after each section to monitor students' comprehension.

- After each section, ask volunteers to tell you something about what they just read.
- Ask a volunteer to tell you the main idea of each section.

Reflect on the Article After reading the article, review ideas introduced before or during reading.

- Ask students to reread their answers to questions in the Real-Life Connection.
- Would their answers be different now that they have read the article? Why or why not?
- Have students complete the K-W-L Chart.

Practice and Apply

Discuss the Questions Gauge students' comprehension and help them develop critical reading skills. (Answer Key, p. 118)

Connect to the Big Question Have students use the Two-Column Journal to focus on the BQ.

- Have students write the Article BQ on their graphic organizers.
- Have students summarize the article. Then have students fill in their thoughts.
- Tell students they can answer the BQ by turning their answer in the *My Thoughts* column of their chart into complete sentences.

Assess

Use this informal assessment before moving on to the Writing Journal activities. Students should answer these questions:

- What does sports have to do with this article?
- Do you think sports are the only activities in which parents can put too much pressure on students? Explain.

Reach All Learners

Build Fluency Choose a section from the article for group reading.

- Read the section to students. Explain to students that part of reading fluently is not to read word-for-word, but to read phrases with expression.
- Have students read along with you.
- Direct one student to read the first sentence. Help the student read with fluency. Repeat this process with other students and sentences.
- As a group, read the section again at a quicker pace.

Use Small Groups Have students generate a Code of Behavior to engage students in active learning.

- Place students in groups of four.
- Have each group write a Code of Behavior for parents who go to their children's games or practices.
- When students are finished, have each group share their rules. Find out if different groups came up with similar rules.

Assist Students Having Difficulty If students struggle to answer the Find It questions, help them by asking the following questions:

- Find It 1: Scan the article. Where do you see the word *pierce*?
- Find It 2: Scan the headings. Where do you see the word *benefits*?
- Find It 3: Scan the headings. What words tell you whether the section will be about a parent who behave badly or a parent who behaves well?

WRITING JOURNAL

Extend

Write About It Students will write a letter to parents of kids in a recreation program.

- Read and discuss the Writing Prompt. (Journal, p. 48) Review the Writing Rubric. Encourage students to add more points to the rubric to guide their work.
- Model how to use the organizer.
- Students should use the Check It and Fix It Section and Writing Checklist to revise and evaluate their work.

Teaching Tip Explain that there are a variety of ways to mark text, including highlighting, underlining, and sticky notes. Give the students some sticky notes and tell them to mark the places in the text that support their arguments. Then they can go back and makes notes on what they marked.

Vocabulary Workshop Students extend their thinking about Word Bank words.

- Students work in pairs or small groups on the Define It organizer. (Journal, p. 50)
- Have students add words to the Your Choice box and their personal word bank.
- Use the Show You Know exercise to assess students' understanding.

Model drafting by thinking aloud:

> **THINK ALOUD** *One of the vocabulary words is* competition. *I will use it as the topic of my first sentence in the dialogue. The first thing that comes into my head is an essay competition. My sentence will be "Are you going to write a story for the school essay competition?"*

The Kindness of Kin

PROGRAM RESOURCES

ANTHOLOGY pp. 56–59

TEACHING GUIDE AND RESOURCES
- Web Map **p. 156**
- Main Idea Map **p. 146**
- Answer Key **p. 118**

REAL WORLD WRITING JOURNAL pp. 52–55

ANTHOLOGY

Preteach

Activate Prior Knowledge Take a poll of *true* and *false* questions in the Real-Life Connection. Students will revisit answers after they read.

Build Background *The 2000 U.S. Census reported that six million children live in a household with a relative other than parents. In some of these households, the parents are present; but in others the relative is the primary caregiver.*

Introduce Vocabulary Help students apply the definitions in the Word Bank. Ask questions such as:

- When have you **assumed** something?
- Describe a **challenge** you have faced.
- *Build Academic Vocabulary* Ask students which Word Bank words can have a good or bad association. For example, many people like a *challenge*, while others find a *challenge* unpleasant.

Teach

Focus on the Big Question Ask the Article BQ, "When people make sacrifices to become kinship parents, do they win or lose?" Students will answer this question after reading.

- *Connect to the Unit Big Question* Write the Unit and Article BQs on the board. Make sure students understand the term *sacrifice*. Ask students if a sacrifice is always a loss.

Preread the Article Before students read, have a class discussion about kinship parents.

- How many students live, or know someone who lives, with a grandparent?
- Turn students' attention to the title, photograph, and caption on the first page of the article. Ask students to tell what they think the article will be about based on these text features.

Conduct a Guided Reading Read the article to the students as they follow along. Pause after each section to monitor students' comprehension.

- Who can be a kinship parent?
- Why might birth parents not be able to care for their children? Model a possible answer:

> **THINK ALOUD** *The article describes an aunt and a sister who became kinship parents. That must mean that any relative willing to take on the responsibility can become a kinship parent. One of them became a kinship parent because the parents were not able to parent at first, and then the parents disappeared. The other became a kinship parent to her sister because their birth mother was not a very good parent.*

Reflect on the Article After reading the article, review ideas introduced before or during reading.

- Retake the poll from the Real-Life Connection. Have the answers changed?
- Ask students why they did or did not change their answers.

Practice and Apply

Discuss the Questions Gauge students' comprehension and help them develop critical reading skills. (Answer Key, p. 118)

Connect to the Big Question Use the Web Map to have students focus on the BQ.

- Have students write the Article BQ on their organizers. In the central oval they should write *Kinship Parents.*
- Discuss some of the pros and cons of becoming a kinship parent. Have students add answers to the graphic organizer.
- Invite volunteers to answer the BQ. Ask them to support their opinions with reasons.

Assess

Have students create a learning log for you to informally assess. Students should answer these questions:

- What was today's article about?
- What is a kinship parent?
- What is one new word you learned?
- What surprised you?

Reach All Learners

Build Fluency Choose a section from the article and instruct students to do a Group Reading to practice fluency.

- Have students read the section silently.
- Direct one student to read the first sentence. Help the student use the correct emphasis and tone to signal the end of the sentence.
- Have the next student read the next sentence. Repeat the process with the entire group.
- Have students read the section again as a group.

Use Small Groups Use the RCRC (Read, Cover, Retell, Check) method to help students assess their own comprehension.

- Place students in groups of four. Give each student in each group a short section of the article to read.
- Explain the process of RCRC to students:
  Read the text.
  Cover it up.
  Retell what they have just read.
  Check to see if they were correct.
- Have each group practice RCRC until all four students have had a chance to test their comprehension.

Assist Students Having Difficulty If students struggle to keep track of main ideas in the article, work with them to fill out the Main Idea Map. Allow time after reading the article to go over the organizer using an overhead transparency.

WRITING JOURNAL

Extend

Write About It Students will write a list of qualities a kinship parent should have.

- Read and discuss the Writing Prompt. (Journal, p. 52) Review the Writing Rubric. Encourage students to add more points to the rubric to guide their work.
- Model how to use the organizer.
- Students should use the Check It and Fix It Section and Writing Checklist to revise and evaluate their work.

Model revising by thinking aloud:

THINK ALOUD *I want to be sure that my sentences are all complete, so I read what I have written out loud. When I stumble over something or have to reread a sentence, I double-check that the grammar is correct. Is it a complete sentence? Have I remembered my periods? Is it a run-on sentence or a sentence fragment? I fix the sentence so that it makes sense when I read it out loud.*

Vocabulary Workshop Students extend their thinking about Word Bank words.

- Students work in pairs or small groups on the Define It organizer. (Journal, p. 54)
- Have students add words to the Your Choice box and their personal word bank.
- Use the Show You Know exercise to assess students' understanding.

Teaching Tip Have the class brainstorm more words and synonyms in the Word Play exercise. Write the words *walk* and *strut* on the board. Have volunteers walk and strut. Explain that even though the two words are synonyms, they have slightly different meanings. Have students come up with other synonyms for *walk* and act out the movement in the class. Discuss how these more descriptive words can add sparkle to their writing.

Sister Champions

PROGRAM RESOURCES

ANTHOLOGY pp. 60–63

TEACHING GUIDE AND RESOURCES
- Making Personal Connections Organizer **p. 147**
- Answer Key **p. 118**

REAL WORLD WRITING JOURNAL pp. 56–59

ANTHOLOGY

Preteach

Activate Prior Knowledge Have students fill out the information in the Real-Life Connection. Students will revisit answers after they read.

Build Background *Professional tennis is played in tournaments around the world. A tournament is a series of matches where only the winners continue to play. One of the most famous tournaments is called the U.S. Open. This tournament takes place every year at the Arthur Ashe Stadium in Flushing, New York.*

Introduce Vocabulary

- Write the Word Bank words on the board. Have students tell you which Word Bank words they have already learned and what they mean.
- Have students use all the vocabulary words in a sentence.
- *Build Academic Vocabulary* Identify academic vocabulary in the Word Bank. Ask how students might use the words *conflict* and *opposition* in other subject areas.

Teach

Focus on the Big Question Ask the Article BQ, "When siblings compete, does anyone win?" Students will answer this question after reading.

- *Connect to the Unit Big Question* Ask students whether they have ever played a game against a sibling. What happened? Did someone's feelings get hurt? Was it fun? Why or why not?

Preread the Article Ask the class the following questions.

- Has anyone ever played tennis or watched tennis?
- Has anyone heard of Venus and Serena Williams? What do you know about them?

Conduct a Guided Reading Read the article to the students as they follow along. Pause after each section to monitor students' comprehension.

- Remind students that part of being a good reader is asking questions.
- Model for students by doing a Think Aloud:

> **THINK ALOUD** *I have a question about when the Williams sisters started playing. I skimmed the page. The article does not say exactly when they started playing, but it was before they turned fourteen.*

Reflect on the Article After reading the article, review ideas introduced before or during reading.

- Have students reread their answers from the Real-Life Connection. Were their ideas about the article correct? Have them change their notes to reflect learning.
- Ask students whether knowing (or learning) things about tennis before they read the article helped them understand.

Practice and Apply

Discuss the Questions Gauge students' comprehension and help them develop critical reading skills. (Answer Key, p. 118)

Connect to the Big Question Have students use the Making Personal Connections Organizer to focus on the BQ.

- Have students write the Article BQ on their organizers. Guide students to use the notes in their graphic organizers to help them answer the BQ.

Assess

Have each student verbally summarize the article to partners. Listen to the conversations to assess understanding. The summary should include:

- Who the article is about
- Why they are famous
- The main idea of the article

Reach All Learners

Build Fluency Choose a section from the article and instruct students to do a Group Reading to practice fluency.

- Put students in groups of four. Have one student in each group read aloud one line from the text. Then have the next student read the second line.
- Direct the students to take turns as seamlessly as possible in their reading.
- If any student has difficulty with a word or line, then have the entire group repeat the sentence aloud until all students are comfortable saying it.

Use Small Groups Have students participate in a group discussion to help answer the Use Clues questions.

- Place students in small groups. Have students choose one of the three Use Clues questions to discuss.
- Ask students to write their answer to the Use Clues question on a piece of paper. Have groups exchange their answers with another group. Repeat until all groups have answered all questions. Discuss the answers with the class.

Assist Students Having Difficulty If students struggle with writing notes, remind students that notes do not have to be complete sentences.

- Work with students to make a list of abbreviations to use when taking notes. Write the abbreviations on the board.
- Model for students examples of taking notes for different activities in the lesson.

WRITING JOURNAL

Extend

Write About It Students will write a speech about Venus and Serena Williams.

- Read and discuss the Writing Prompt. (Journal, p. 56) Review the Writing Rubric. Encourage students to add more points to the rubric to guide their work.
- Model how to use the organizer.
- Students should use the Check It and Fix It Section and Writing Checklist to revise and evaluate their work.

Model drafting by thinking aloud:

> **THINK ALOUD** *I want to be sure that each sentence includes an important idea to support my opinion. I will put my strongest argument last so that my readers remember it. A phrase such as* in conclusion *signals that I am ending the letter with a strong idea.*

Vocabulary Workshop Students extend their thinking about Word Bank words.

- Students work in pairs or small groups on the Define It organizer. (Journal, p. 58)
- Have students add words to the Your Choice box and their personal word bank.
- Use the Show You Know exercise to assess students' understanding.

Teaching Tip Have groups of students act out each word in the Word Bank. Have volunteers tell what word students are acting out. Encourage another volunteer to use the word in a sentence. Continue until all groups have had a chance to act out at least one word.

UNIT 2

Two Views of the Zoo

PROGRAM RESOURCES

ANTHOLOGY pp. 64–67

TEACHING GUIDE AND RESOURCES
- Word Pyramid **p. 157**
- Main Idea Map **p. 146**
- Answer Key **p. 119**

REAL WORLD WRITING JOURNAL pp. 60–63

ANTHOLOGY

Preteach

Activate Prior Knowledge Help students fill out the rating chart in the Real-Life Connection. Then have students set a purpose for reading.

Build Background *There are more than 2,000 animal exhibitors in the United States. Only 10 percent of these exhibitors are accredited by the American Zoo and Aquarium Association. When something is accredited, it has been examined to be sure that it is safe for animals and visitors.*

Introduce Vocabulary

- Have students work in pairs to read the Word Bank words and definitions to each other.
- Then have each pair find the boldface words in the selection.
- Help students fill out the Word Pyramid for each word.
- *Build Academic Vocabulary* Write the academic vocabulary words on the board. Ask students how they might use these words in a science or math class. Have students write sentences using the words to describe a math problem and its *outcome*.

Teach

Focus on the Big Question Ask the Article BQ, "Should animals be put in zoos?" Students will answer this question after reading.

- *Connect to the Unit Big Question* Have students discuss why the Article BQ might cause a conflict.

Preread the Article Before students read the entire article, have them read the first sentence of each paragraph. Then have students predict what the article will be about.

Conduct a Guided Reading Read the article to the students as they follow along. Pause after each section to monitor students' comprehension. Ask volunteers to summarize each view.

Reflect on the Article After reading the article, review ideas introduced before or during reading.

- Have students write what they now know about each point in the Real-Life Connection chart.
- Have students answer the questions they posed for themselves before they read the article.
- Discuss whether students' predictions were accurate. Model checking predictions:

> **THINK ALOUD** *I thought I knew everything about zoos and endangered species before I read this article, but I learned a lot. I had never thought about zoos saving endangered species. Now I think differently about zoos.*

Practice and Apply

Discuss the Questions Gauge students' comprehension and help them develop critical reading skills. (Answer Key, p. 119)

Connect to the Big Question Have students use the Main Idea Map to focus on the BQ.

- Have students write the Article BQ on their organizers. Ask questions that will guide them to find the main idea.
- After students have completed their graphic organizers, call on volunteers to answer the BQ. Ask them to support their opinions with reasons from the article.

Assess

Have students answer these questions for you to informally assess their understanding.

- What did you learn about in class today?
- Think about a visit you may have taken to a zoo or a zoo you have heard or read about.
- Which "view of the zoo" did you see on your visit? Explain how your experience matches one of these views.

Reach All Learners

Build Fluency Choose a section from the article for a Paired Reading.

- Pair students and have them read silently.
- Direct one student to read aloud while the other follows along, making notes.
- The listener provides suggestions and feedback. Students then reverse roles.

Use Small Groups Engage students with a Write-Around activity.

- Put students in small groups and give each a piece of paper with the third Use Clues question written across the top.
- Have students write a response for one minute and then pass their papers to the right. The one-minute writing begins again, and students add to the paper in front of them, responding to the idea that is already there.
- Continue until all students in the group have written on each paper.

Assist Students Having Difficulty If students struggle to keep track of the points of view in the article, ask them to visualize.

- Ask students to describe what an "old zoo" looked like. Then have students describe what a "new zoo" looks like.
- Ask students to imagine an animal that does not like being in a zoo. How does the animal look? What is the animal doing?
- Next, ask students to imagine an animal that is safe and protected in a modern zoo. What does it look like? What is it doing?

WRITING JOURNAL

Extend

Write About It Students will write a blog about whether animals should be in zoos.

- Read and discuss the Writing Prompt. (Journal, p. 60) Review the Writing Rubric. Encourage students to add more points to the rubric to guide their work.
- Model how to use the organizer.
- Students should use the Check It and Fix It Section and Writing Checklist to revise and evaluate their work.

Model revising by thinking aloud:

> **THINK ALOUD** *I want to be sure that my argument is powerful. I will check what I have written to see if I have made interesting and specific word choices. I see that my second sentence is "Putting animals in zoos is not nice." That sentence seems flat. I will change it to read "Putting animals in zoos may seem cruel." That is a more powerful sentence.*

Vocabulary Workshop Students extend their thinking about Word Bank words.

- Students work in pairs or small groups on the Define It organizer. (Journal, p. 62)
- Have students add words to the Your Choice box and their personal word bank.
- Use the Show You Know exercise to assess students' understanding.

Teaching Tip Work with students to combine all the prefixes with the root words. Tell students that *operate* can mean "to work." Therefore, *cooperation* means "to work together." Help students with the root word meaning for *compromise*.

UNIT 2

Either Too Young or Too Old

PROGRAM RESOURCES

ANTHOLOGY pp. 68–71

TEACHING GUIDE AND RESOURCES
- Venn Diagram p. 154
- Answer Key p. 119

REAL WORLD WRITING JOURNAL pp. 64–67

ANTHOLOGY

Preteach

Activate Prior Knowledge Take a poll of *true* or *false* for each question in the Real-Life Connection. Students will revisit answers after they read.

Build Background *The 26th Amendment, setting the voting age at eighteen, was passed in 1971 because of the military draft and the Vietnam War. People felt that if someone was old enough to serve in the military and die for their country, he was old enough to vote.*

Introduce Vocabulary

- Review the Word Bank definitions and sample sentences. Ask student pairs to have a dialogue using the words.
- Choose a volunteer to help you model the activity for students. For example, *I had a misunderstanding with my best friend and both of us got angry. We needed better communication.*
- *Build Academic Vocabulary* Write the academic vocabulary words on the board. Have students work together to use the words to describe a historical or current event.

Teach

Focus on the Big Question Ask the Article BQ, "Is there a 'right age' to start voting or stop working?" Students will answer this question after reading.

- *Connect to the Unit Big Question* Write the Article BQ on the board. Discuss with students the conflict involved in the question. Ask students how this question connects to the Unit BQ.

Preread the Article Before students read, have them read the Wrap It Up questions. Based on these questions, have them predict what they will find out about voting. Model how to predict:

THINK ALOUD *Five of the questions have to do with a person's age. One question asks about the knowledge needed to vote. One asks about the age of workers. I'm predicting that the article will be about how old or young a person needs to be to vote or work.*

Conduct a Guided Reading Read the article to the students as they follow along. Pause after each section to monitor students' comprehension.

- Ask students to identify the main idea of each section.
- Ask a volunteer to give his or her opinion about the views expressed in each section.

Reflect on the Article After reading the article, review ideas introduced before or during reading.

- Retake the poll from the Real-Life Connection. Have students' answers changed? Ask why or why not.
- Ask students if their predictions about the article were correct.

Practice and Apply

Discuss the Questions Gauge students' comprehension and help them develop critical reading skills. (Answer Key, p. 119)

Connect to the Big Question Have students use the Venn Diagram to focus on the BQ.

- Have students write the Article BQ on their organizers and label the ovals *Vote* and *Work*.
- Have students summarize the two issues in each oval. In the center, ask students to list similarities between the issues.
- Encourage students to use their graphic organizers to answer the BQ.

Assess

Use this informal assessment before moving on to the Writing Journal activities. Students should answer these three questions:

- What was the *subject* of today's article?
- What is one new word in today's reading? How would you use it?
- Give an example of a time you compromised. Link your personal connection to the article.

Reach All Learners

Build Fluency Choose a section from the article for Paired Reading.

- Have students read the section in pairs and coach each other on fluency. Tell students that if disagreements arise, they should ask for your help.
- Then have each student read aloud one or two lines from the section to the entire class.

Use Small Groups Use a discussion activity to engage students in active learning.

- In groups of four, have students discuss what issues might prompt them to vote.
- Have students write notes during the discussion.
- After the discussion have each student answer the third Use Clues question.

Assist Students Having Difficulty If students struggle to remember what they read, provide them with an outline to refer to.

- The outline should include the article title and any subheads with space for notes.
- Direct students to fill in the outline as they read.
- Allow time after reading the article to go over the outline using an overhead transparency.

WRITING JOURNAL

Extend

Write About It Students will write a letter about lowering the voting age.

- Read and discuss the Writing Prompt. (Journal, p. 64) Review the Writing Rubric. Encourage students to add more points to the rubric to guide their work.
- Model how to use the organizer.
- Students should use the Check It and Fix It Section and Writing Checklist to revise and evaluate their work.

Teaching Tip Have the class brainstorm ways that the Word Bank words could be used in their letters. Show the class the basic format for writing a letter.

Vocabulary Workshop Students extend their thinking about Word Bank words.

- Students work in pairs or small groups on the Define It organizer. (Journal, p. 66)
- Have students add words to the Your Choice box and their personal word bank.
- Use the Show You Know exercise to assess students' understanding.

Think aloud as you model creating clues for the words:

> **THINK ALOUD** *If I am having trouble coming up with a clue for a word, I might start by turning the definition into a question. For example, I might say, "What is a word that describes sharing thoughts or feelings?"*

UNIT 2 WRAP UP

Does every conflict have a winner?

Introduce the Unit Project

Debate Students will participate in a debate, choosing and presenting an answer to the Big Question: *Does every conflict have a winner?*

- Read through the steps of the assignment with students.
- Point out the rubric so that students will know their goals for the assignment. Add other rubric points with students to guide their work.
- Instruct students on the rules of polite debate.
- Allow time for students to practice and present the debate. Encourage listeners to offer their feedback and advice on debate arguments.

Model Model how to strengthen an argument by thinking aloud:

> **THINK ALOUD** *As I think about my debate topic, I realize that one of my arguments is not very convincing, so I am going to toss it out. I would rather have a few really strong points than many weak ones. The debate arguments I have left are good ones, but I am going to put them in order. The least convincing point will be first, and then each point will get stronger. Then my audience will be left with the strongest idea.*

Teaching Tip Transitions, such as *first, most important, in conclusion,* and so on, will help students organize their ideas. Brainstorm transitions with students. Leave a list on the board or chart paper for students' reference.

Conclude the Unit

Review Unit Objectives Return to the unit objectives and ask students to evaluate how well they mastered each one on a scale of 1 to 5, with 1 being low and 5 being high. Discuss how lower scores could be improved.

Reflect on the Learning Examine the bulletin board with students. Ask them to reflect on what they have learned. They can write or discuss with the class or in small groups. Prompt students' thinking with questions such as:

- What was the most interesting article you read? What did you like about it?
- How did your ideas about conflict change as you read through the articles?
- Which topic would you like to know more about? What do you still wonder about it?
- How did the writing assignments and the debate help you form your ideas about conflict?
- What other article topics do you think could be included in this unit? How would those topics help people learn about conflict?

Name _____

Word Bank Quiz

WORD LIST A			
assume	communication	disagreement	prepare
attitude	competition	obstacle	style
challenge	desire	perform	understanding

Ten of the unit Word Bank words are defined in parentheses in the article below. As you read the article, use Word List A, above, to figure out which word best fits each definition. Write the word on the line provided. (You will not use every word on the list.) Then go on to the next page of the quiz.

A Football Announcement

The final **(1. contest between individuals)** _____ for spots on

the football team is on Friday. Players from last year's team should not **(2. suppose**

something is true without checking to make sure) _____

that they will get on this year's team. Players have to have a **(3. strong need)**

_____ to get on the team. You are expected to have a positive

(4. way of thinking and feeling about things) _____.

(5. A particular way of doing something or expressing yourself)

_____ is not the key to getting on this team. You need good

(6. sharing of information or feeling) _____ skills. You need to

have a strong **(7. knowledge of the meaning)** _____ of football.

Every player will be expected to **(8. get ready)** _____ for games by

coming to practice. If you like a **(9. thing that is difficult)** _____

and can face any **(10. thing that blocks paths)** _____, then you are

right for this team.

UNIT 2 Word Bank Quiz

WORD LIST B			
compromise	desire	outcome	struggle
conflict	misunderstanding	plan	subject
danger	opposition	resolution	understanding

Ten more Word Bank words are defined in parentheses in the article below. As you read the article, use Word List B, above, to figure out which word best fits each definition. Write the word on the line provided. (You will not use every word on the list.)

No More Fights!

When I was little, my brother and I had a **(11. argument or clash)**

_____ about nearly every **(12. topic)** _____

on earth. We both wanted our way, so it was hard for us to **(13. give something up**

in order to settle an argument) _____. We did not listen to each

other either, so even a simple **(14. wrong idea about what somebody said or meant)**

_____ could lead to a fight. One day we were so busy arguing that

we did not see a **(15. thing that was unsafe)** _____ right in front of

us. We were ready to cross the street, and my brother did not notice a car passing by!

That was it for my mother. She came up with a **(16. method or way)**

_____ to end our fights. Unless we could figure out a

(17. way to end our conflict) _____, we would no longer be

able to play at the park every day. We immediately voiced our **(18. resistance)**

_____. However, my mother won in the end. We both had to

(19. try hard) _____ to stop fighting, but we did. The **(20. final**

result) _____ was that my brother and I got along better.

We wanted our time at the park!

UNIT 3

What should we learn?

Unit Overview

The articles in this unit explore the topic of what we need to learn. As students read about different explorations and investigations, they will discuss what learning new things can mean to them and to society as a whole.

Launch the Unit

Connect to the Big Question Read the introduction with students and examine the illustration. Ask questions such as:

- *What are some things that people learn every day and in special situations?*
- *Describe the learning situation in the illustration.*
- *What does the person in the illustration need to learn?*
- *What connections do you have to this situation?*
- *What would you like to learn more about? How would this information help you?*

Use the prompt on the page as the basis for journal writing or for small group or whole class discussion. Students can share their ideas with partners or in small groups.

Anchor Students' Thinking Start a bulletin board on which you post the Big Question. Throughout the unit, students can add to the bulletin board. Use ideas such as the following:

- Ask students what they are learning about in other classes. Students can post interesting topics or facts.
- Have students bring articles and photographs from newspapers, Web sites, or magazines that contain information they think the class might like to learn.
- Place exemplary writing from students' writing journal assignments on the bulletin board. Discuss with students what these writings say about learning.
- Encourage students to add other examples of things they think we should learn about. Link students' findings to ideas in the articles and to the Unit Big Question.

Unit Objectives

Share these objectives with students. As you read the articles in this unit, you will:

- Identify different types of things people need to learn.
- Determine an answer to the Big Question: *What should we learn?* Explain your answers using details from the articles and from your own experiences.
- Use vocabulary words to talk and write about learning.
- Form an opinion for a poster and support that opinion with facts.

UNIT 3

Travel to Mars

PROGRAM RESOURCES

ANTHOLOGY pp. 76–79

TEACHING GUIDE AND RESOURCES
- Main Idea Map **p. 146**
- Answer Key **p. 120**

REAL WORLD WRITING JOURNAL pp. 70–73

ANTHOLOGY

Preteach

Activate Prior Knowledge Have students fill out the Real-Life Connection chart. Students will revisit answers after they read.

Build Background *All the heat in the solar system comes from the sun. Planets that are closer to the sun are too hot for life. Planets that are farther away are too cold. Mars is the fourth planet from the sun. Its thin atmosphere creates huge extremes in temperature on the planet.*

Introduce Vocabulary

- Have students read the words and definitions in the Word Bank. Ask volunteers to act out the three verbs: *discover, explore, organize.*
- Make statements such as "It could rain tomorrow," and "Today is Monday." Have students respond with either "That's possible" or "That's a fact."
- *Build Academic Vocabulary* All of the words in the Word Bank are academic vocabulary. Ask students to identify words that they might use in other school subjects. Have students work in pairs to write a sentence for each word.

Teach

Focus on the Big Question Ask the Article BQ, "What do we need to learn about Mars to live there?" Students will answer this question after reading.

- *Connect to the Unit Big Question* Write the Unit and Article BQs on the board. With students, circle similar words and ideas to show how the BQs are linked.

Preread the Article Before students read, model how to preview the article and ask questions about it:

| THINK ALOUD | *This is an interesting title, "Travel to Mars."* |

Even before I read the article, I know that we cannot travel to Mars yet. So I have a question to answer as I read: Is travel to Mars going to be possible in the future? I think the article will help me answer that question.

Model how to come up with a question to keep in mind as you read. Then ask students to come up with other questions about the article.

Conduct a Guided Reading Read the article to the students as they follow along. Pause after each section to monitor students' comprehension.

- Have students pause to ask questions as they read.
- Have students make connections to facts they already know about space.

Reflect on the Article After reading the article, review ideas introduced before or during reading.

- Review the chart in the Real-Life Connection. Have answers changed? Why or why not?
- Ask students whether they made changes to their predictions. Have them explain why.

Practice and Apply

Discuss the Questions Gauge students' comprehension and help them develop critical reading skills. (Answer Key, p. 120)

Connect to the Big Question Refocus students' attention on the Article BQ.

- Have groups discuss the obstacles to living on Mars by referring to the article. Ask groups to add other obstacles that they foresee.
- Then ask students to create a list of questions with what we need to learn before we can live on Mars.

Assess

Use this informal assessment before moving on to the Writing Journal activities. Have students write a short summary of the article. To prepare, have students use the Main Idea Map to write the main idea of the article and supporting ideas. Remind them that a good summary includes only the most important ideas.

Reach All Learners

Build Fluency Focus on the imaginary advertisement at the beginning of the article. Have students read the ad as though they were on the radio in order to practice fluency.

- Read aloud to model reading with correct expression.
- Have students select a section and read aloud to a partner.
- After students have had the opportunity to read several times, ask for volunteers to read their section to the class.

Use Small Groups Engage students with a Write-Around activity for the first Use Clues question.

- In groups of four, have each student begin with a piece of paper with the first Use Clues question written across the top.
- Have students write a response for one minute and then pass their papers to the right. The one-minute writing begins again, and students add to the paper in front of them.
- Continue until all four students have written on each paper. Share writing in a class discussion.

Assist Students Having Difficulty If students struggle to come up with prereading questions, have a brainstorming session.

- Ask students what they would like to know about travel to Mars.
- Help them to formulate their statements into questions.

WRITING JOURNAL

Extend

Write About It Students will write a postcard to a friend.

- Read and discuss the Writing Prompt. (Journal, p. 70) Review the Writing Rubric.
- Encourage students to add more points to the rubric to guide their work.
- Model how to use the organizer.
- Students should use the Check It and Fix It Section and Writing Checklist to revise and evaluate their work.

Model adding details to writing by thinking aloud:

THINK ALOUD *I am writing a postcard as though I were living on Mars. That means I will need to use my personal experience of daily life and what people do. I will also need to have information about Mars. That is where the article comes in.*

Vocabulary Workshop Students extend their thinking about Word Bank words.

- Students work in pairs or small groups on the Define It organizer. (Journal, p. 73)
- Have students add words to the Your Choice box and their personal word bank.
- Use the Show You Know exercise to assess students' understanding.

Teaching Tip Create a Word Wall that you will use throughout this unit. Have a volunteer write each Word Bank word on a board or chart paper. As you do each activity in the Writing Journal, have a student add the words you learn to the Word Wall.

UNIT 3

Look Who's Talking

PROGRAM RESOURCES

ANTHOLOGY pp. 80–83

TEACHING GUIDE AND RESOURCES
- Opinion and Reasons Organizer **p. 148**
- Answer Key **p. 120**

REAL WORLD WRITING JOURNAL pp. 74–77

ANTHOLOGY

Preteach

Activate Prior Knowledge Take a poll for each pair of statements in the Real-Life Connection. Students will revisit answers after they read.

Build Background *Some differences between people are qualities they are born with. Other differences come from the way people are treated by their families and society. When people are treated equally, the differences are smaller.*

Introduce Vocabulary

- Read aloud the sentences from the article in which boldface vocabulary words appear. Discuss what each word means in context.
- Give students the opportunity to practice the words in a new context. Work with students to create new sentences for each word.
- *Build Academic Vocabulary* Write the academic vocabulary words on the board. Discuss with students how they might use *analyze, investigate,* and *topic* in other subject areas.

Teach

Focus on the Big Question Ask the Article BQ, "What can we learn from differences in speaking styles?" Students will answer this question after reading.

- *Connect to the Unit Big Question* Write the Unit and Article BQs on the board. Ask for the difference between what we should learn and what we can learn about this subject.

Preread the Article Before students read, discuss with them the difference between a fact and an opinion. Invite a volunteer to read the pullout quote on p. 82. Take a poll of how many students agree with either or both of those statements. Ask whether they think information in the article might change their minds.

Conduct a Guided Reading Read the article to students as they follow along. Pause after each section to monitor students' comprehension.

- Have students discuss whether the statements they are reading are facts or opinions.
- Ask students whether they agree. Model how to form and support an opinion:

> **THINK ALOUD** *The article says that some people think boys and girls have trouble understanding each other because of the way they talk. I do not know whether I agree with those people. That is their opinion, but I wonder if they have any facts to support it. I will keep reading to find out.*

Reflect on the Article After reading the article, review ideas introduced before or during reading.

- Retake the poll from the Real-Life Connection. Have answers changed? Ask students why.
- Ask students to formulate a new opinion.

Practice and Apply

Discuss the Questions Gauge students' comprehension and help them develop critical reading skills. (Answer Key, p. 120)

Connect to the Big Question Have students use the Opinion and Reasons Organizer to answer the BQ.

- Have students write the Article BQ on their organizers. Give them examples of how they could answer it, from "strongly agree" to "strongly disagree."
- Ask volunteers to answer the BQ. Students should support their opinions with reasons based on the article and the class discussion.

Assess

Have students work in groups to write a short dialogue about a dish to be added to the cafeteria menu. The characters in the dialogue should be named Boy and Girl. Then whisper to each group either to cast a girl to read the boy's lines and a boy to read the girl's lines or to cast according to the way they lines were written. Have the groups present their dialogues. After each, have the class discuss what they learned from the experiment, referring to what they learned from the article.

Reach All Learners

Build Fluency Divide the class into groups of four or five. Choose a section from the article and instruct students to do a Round Robin Reading to practice fluency.

- Tell students that punctuation gives them clues to how words should be read.
- Have one student begin by reading the first sentence of the section. The student at his or her right will read the second, continuing until the entire section has been read.
- Ask students to think about how they could improve their reading and begin the section again, with another student reading the first sentence.

Use Small Groups Use a "numbered heads together" activity to increase peer teaching. Give the class one of the Use Clues questions.

- Organize students into groups of four. Count off one through four.
- After a brief time for discussion, ask all the number threes to stand if they know the answer to the question. If any of them do not know, go back to discussion time.
- Continue the activity until all members of all groups have had the opportunity to answer.

Assist Students Having Difficulty If students have trouble with the idea of speaking styles, make a comparison to something more familiar, such as music or clothing.

- Play two different kinds of music. Ask students to describe the differences between the two.
- Show students photographs of different styles of clothing and have them discuss the differences.

WRITING JOURNAL

Extend

Write About It Students will write a checklist for a language expert.

- Read and discuss the Writing Prompt. (Journal, p. 74) Review the Writing Rubric.
- Encourage students to add more points to the rubric to guide their work.
- Model how to use the organizer.
- Students should use the Check It and Fix It Section and Writing Checklist to revise and evaluate their work.

Model drafting by thinking aloud:

> **THINK ALOUD** *I think a checklist for research is a little like a true/false test. I do not have to agree with everything I write. I am going to write sentences that might or might not be true, like "Girls speak more politely." It will be up to the person who is doing the research to find out whether that is true.*

Vocabulary Workshop Students extend their thinking about Word Bank words.

- Students work in pairs or small groups on the Define It organizer. (Journal, p. 76)
- Have students add words to the Your Choice box and their personal word bank.
- Use the Show You Know exercise to assess students' understanding.

Teaching Tip After doing the Multiple Meaning activity, ask students to brainstorm other multiple meaning words. As a challenge, ask for volunteers to use a word twice in a sentence, each time with a different meaning. Example: "I mean that you are really mean."

Making Sport of Tradition

PROGRAM RESOURCES

ANTHOLOGY pp. 84–87

TEACHING GUIDE AND RESOURCES
- Two-Column Journal **p. 153**
- Answer Key **p. 120**

REAL WORLD WRITING JOURNAL pp. 78–81

ANTHOLOGY

Preteach

Activate Prior Knowledge Have partners write *true* or *false* for each statement in the Real-Life Connection. Students will revisit answers after they read.

Build Background *The National Collegiate Athletic Association Executive Committee prohibits NCAA colleges and universities from displaying racial, ethnic, or national origin mascots and nicknames or imagery that can be seen as hostile or abusive at any of the 88 NCAA championships.*

Introduce Vocabulary

- Read aloud the sentences from the article in which boldface vocabulary words appear. Discuss what each word means in context.
- Divide students into groups of three or four. Have each group write a sentence using as many of the vocabulary words as they can.
- *Build Academic Vocabulary* Write the academic vocabulary words on index cards. Divide students into small groups and distribute a card to each. Ask groups explain how they might use the word in another subject.

Teach

Focus on the Big Question Ask the Article BQ₂ "Why is it important to learn about cultures different from your own?" Students will answer this question after reading.

- *Connect to the Unit Big Question* Write the Unit and Article BQs on the board. Ask students to think about why learning about other cultures might improve the lives of people in a community or country.

Preread the Article Before students read, model how to preview and predict:

| **THINK ALOUD** | *I am going to look at the headings in the article.* |

I see the words unkind, Native American, *and* sacred ground. *I think this is going to be a serious article. There might be some ideas in the article that I will feel strongly about. I should be ready to use my life experiences to help me understand other people's feelings.*

Ask students to scan the article for other text features and write a prediction about the article.

Conduct a Guided Reading Read the article to the students as they follow along. Pause after each section to monitor students' comprehension.

- Display or distribute the Two-Column Journal.
- Have students fill in the graphic organizer as they read.

Reflect on the Article After reading the article, review ideas introduced before or during reading.

- Have students review their answers to the Real-Life Connection.
- Ask students what new information they learned about Native Americans from the article.

Practice and Apply

Discuss the Questions Gauge students' comprehension and help them develop critical reading skills. (Answer Key, p. 120)

Connect to the Big Question Refocus students' attention on the Article BQ.

- Ask students to think again about some things they know about other cultures.
- Divide the class into small groups and have students discuss mascots, nicknames, and imagery that might hurt their feelings or those of people they know.

Assess

Have students summarize the article in their own words for you to informally assess understanding. Remind students that a good summary includes a topic sentence that tells what the article was about. Encourage students to provide details they recall from the article in their summaries.

Reach All Learners

Build Fluency Choose a section from the article for Paired Reading.

- Pair students and have them read silently.
- Direct one student to read the section aloud while the other follows along, making notes.
- The listener provides suggestions and feedback. Students then reverse roles.

Use Small Groups Use an art activity to engage students in active learning.

- Have students work in small groups to create an image or nickname that is sensitive to cultures.
- Tell groups that each member of the group should contribute ideas, even though only one or two may actually draw the image.
- Have each group present mascot images to the class. Discuss the images and display the drawings in the classroom.

Assist Students Having Difficulty If students have difficulty pinpointing context clues for the vocabulary words, allow them to simply write the sentence in which the word appears.

- Talk through the context as a class.
- Emphasize that context simply adds to what you already know about a word and that context will not always help with the meaning of a word. In that case, students should turn to a dictionary or the Word Bank definitions.

WRITING JOURNAL

Extend

Write About It Students will write a letter to the principal of a school.

- Read and discuss the Writing Prompt. (Journal, p. 78) Review the Writing Rubric.
- Encourage students to add more points to the rubric to guide their work.
- Model how to use the organizer.
- Students should use the Check It and Fix It Section and Writing Checklist to revise and evaluate their work.

Teaching Tip If students have difficulty with the Show You Know activity, have them work in pairs and write alternate lines of dialogue. Reading dialogue aloud will help students determine if it sounds natural.

Vocabulary Workshop Students extend their thinking about Word Bank words.

- Students work in pairs or small groups on the Define It organizer. (Journal, p. 80)
- Have students add words to the Your Choice box and their personal word bank.
- Use the Show You Know exercise to assess students' understanding.

Model as you complete the Define It activity:

> **THINK ALOUD** *This is interesting. I am supposed to write what the word means and then what it does not mean. I do not think that means "opposite," because most of these words do not have opposites. The sample says that* evaluate *does not mean "adding or subtracting numbers." I guess that is something you might think it means, but it does not. Someone might think* inquire *means something like "need." I will put that in.*

UNIT 3

In Your Dreams

PROGRAM RESOURCES

ANTHOLOGY pp. 88–91

TEACHING GUIDE AND RESOURCES
• Web Map p. 156
• Three-Column Chart p. 152
• Answer Key p. 121

REAL WORLD WRITING JOURNAL pp. 82–85

ANTHOLOGY

Preteach

Activate Prior Knowledge Read the Real-Life Connection to students. Have students answer the question.

Build Background *Dreams are not reality and cannot predict future events. They may, however, help us understand our feelings.*

Introduce Vocabulary

• Use the Web Map. Have students put the word *information* in the center circle. Have students put the other three vocabulary words in the outer circles.
• Ask volunteers to explain how each of the outer words relates to the central *information*. Model for students:

> **THINK ALOUD** *How would* curiosity *relate to* information? *Well, I could be curious about all kinds of things. What would satisfy my curiosity? It would be information about those things.*

• *Build Academic Vocabulary* Have volunteers locate words in the Word Bank that might be used when discussing learning. Ask students to explain how examining information might help them to recall the information.

Teach

Focus on the Big Question Ask the Article BQ, "What can we learn from our dreams?" Students will answer this question after reading.

• *Connect to the Unit Big Question* Have students read the Unit and Article BQs. Ask students whether they think it is important to learn about dreams.

Preread the Article Before students read, scan the article title, photos, captions, and boldface words with them. Ask students to predict what they will learn.

Conduct a Guided Reading Read the article to the students as they follow along. Pause after each section to monitor students' comprehension.

• Have students ask a question after reading each section.
• In the final section of the article, discuss the cultural differences of symbols by asking students to add examples.

Reflect on the Article After reading the article, review ideas introduced before or during reading.

• Ask volunteers to share their answers from the Real-Life Connection. Have their answers changed? Why or why not?
• Review students' predictions. Were they accurate?

Practice and Apply

Discuss the Questions Gauge students' comprehension and help them develop critical reading skills. (Answer Key, p. 121)

Connect to the Big Question Use the Three-Column Chart to have students answer the BQ.

• Write this list of symbols on the board: *star, tiger, eagle, moon, cat, tree, fire.* Have students choose three symbols and write them at the top of each column. Below each, have students write words they associate with each symbol.
• Have students choose one symbol and write what they think a dream about it might mean.
• Call on volunteers to answer the BQ. Ask students to support their opinions with reasons based on the article.

Assess

Have students create a Learning Log for you to informally assess. Students should answer these questions:

- What did you learn about dreams?
- What did you find interesting?
- What more would you like to learn about dreams?

Reach All Learners

Build Fluency Choose a section from the article and do a Choral Reading to practice fluency.

- Read the section aloud as students read the section silently.
- Reread the section aloud and have students choral read it with you.
- Then have students choral read the section without you. Stop and correct any pronunciation or fluency errors.

Use Small Groups Engage students with a Write-Around activity.

- In groups of four, have each student begin with a piece of paper with the first Use Clues question written across the top.
- Have students write a response for one minute and then pass their papers to the right. The one-minute writing begins again, and students add to the paper in front of them.
- Continue until all four students have written on each paper. Share writing in a class discussion.

Assist Students Having Difficulty If students struggle to understand longer sentences, show them how to turn long, complex sentences into shorter, more understandable chunks.

- Point out a compound or complex sentence in the selection. Read it aloud as two sentences. Ask students if they can understand the two sentences.
- Read the sentence as it was originally written. Ask students if they understand the whole sentence.

WRITING JOURNAL

Extend

Write About It Students will write about whether or not dreams are meaningful.

- Read and discuss the Writing Prompt. (Journal, p. 82) Review the Writing Rubric.
- Encourage students to add more points to the rubric to guide their work.
- Model how to use the organizer.
- Students should use the Check It and Fix It Section and Writing Checklist to revise and evaluate their work.

Model organizing thoughts for writing as you think aloud:

> **THINK ALOUD** *I have a pretty good idea what my opinion is on this subject, but taking notes on this organizer will help me organize my thoughts. The article says that sleep doctors believe your emotions and memories are active when you sleep. I will put that in the left column because it is a reason that dreams might be meaningful.*

Vocabulary Workshop Students extend their thinking about Word Bank words.

- Students work in pairs or small groups on the Define It organizer. (Journal, p. 84)
- Have students add words to the Your Choice box and their personal word bank.
- Use the Show You Know exercise to assess students' understanding.

Teaching Tip If students struggle with making connections in the Define It activity, allow students to discuss their connections in small groups.

UNIT 3

The Titans Remember

PROGRAM RESOURCES

ANTHOLOGY pp. 92–95

TEACHING GUIDE AND RESOURCES
- Series of Events Map p. 150
- Answer Key p. 121

REAL WORLD WRITING JOURNAL pp. 86–89

ANTHOLOGY

Preteach

Activate Prior Knowledge Have students copy and complete the word web. Ask volunteers to share their word associations with the class. Students will revisit answers after they read.

Build Background *When Gregory Allen Howard, the screenwriter for the movie about the Titans, moved to Alexandria, Virginia, he found the city to be "more socially integrated than anywhere I've ever been or seen." When he asked people why, "they referred back to a football team that brought the city together." That is why Howard wrote the screenplay.*

Introduce Vocabulary

- Divide the class into five groups and assign each group one of the words.
- Have each group work together on a presentation about the word they have been assigned.
- *Build Academic Vocabulary* Ask how students might use the words *analyze* and *background* in other subject areas.

Teach

Focus on the Big Question Ask the Article BQ, "How do people who are different learn to work together?" Students will answer this question after reading.

- *Connect to the Unit Big Question* Have students read the Unit BQ and Article BQ. Ask how they might be related.

Preread the Article Before students read, model how to preview topic sentences and make predictions about content:

THINK ALOUD *I am going to skim the article to make a prediction about what it is about. I can read topic sentences when I preview an article for information. Topic sentences usually contain the main idea for each paragraph.*

Ask students to write a prediction about the article.

Conduct a Guided Reading Read the article to the students as they follow along. Pause after each section to monitor students' comprehension.

- Distribute the Series of Events Map.
- Have students fill in the map as they read.

Reflect on the Article After reading the article, review ideas introduced before or during reading.

- Have students turn to their word webs from the Real-Life Connection. Have them revise their webs by adding or removing words.
- Ask students if they would change their predictions about the article after reading it.

Practice and Apply

Discuss the Questions Gauge students' comprehension and help them develop critical reading skills. (Answer Key, p. 121)

Connect to the Big Question Refocus students' attention on the Article BQ.

- Ask students to talk about some of the ways people from different backgrounds work together in their own community.
- Have students list additional ways in which people might work together to improve community relations.
- Call on volunteers to answer the BQ. Ask students to support their opinions with reasons from the article.

Assess

As a group, discuss with students what they learned from the article with questions such as these:

- Why do people sometimes fear or dislike others who are different?
- What did the Titans learn about the differences of other people?
- What questions would you like to ask the Titans?

Reach All Learners

Build Fluency Divide the class into groups. Choose a section from the article for a Round Robin Reading. Before students read in Round Robin style, be sure they have time to practice.

- Have one student begin by reading the first sentence of the section. The student at his or her right will read the second, continuing until the entire section has been read.
- Ask students to think about how they could improve their reading, and begin with another student reading the first sentence.

Use Small Groups Have students make movie proposals.

- Have students work in small groups to discuss stories that could be made into movies. The stories might be from the news, from your school, or from class reading.
- Each group should focus on one idea and discuss why it would make a good movie.
- The groups should present their proposals to the class. The presentations may include casting possibilities and any other suggestions the students would like to make.

Assist Students Having Difficulty If students have difficulty understanding the racial situation in the United States in 1971, give them a brief explanation of Jim Crow laws.

- The Jim Crow laws were a series of laws enacted by Southern states after Reconstruction that established segregation or separation of the races.
- The Civil Rights Movement and laws passed in 1964 and 1965 helped to overturn the Jim Crow Laws.
- By 1971, many people were still uneasy with the new situation.

WRITING JOURNAL

Extend

Write About It Students will write a paragraph about one lesson learned from the Titans.

- Read and discuss the Writing Prompt. (Journal, p. 86) Review the Writing Rubric.
- Encourage students to add more points to the rubric to guide their work.
- Model how to use the organizer.
- Students should use the Check It and Fix It Section and Writing Checklist to revise and evaluate their work.

Teaching Tip Before students begin working on the organizer, have a class discussion about life lessons. Ask students to talk about lessons they have learned from a parent or coach or teacher, from a friend, or from dealing with siblings. Formulate a definition of "life lesson."

Vocabulary Workshop Students extend their thinking about Word Bank words.

- Students work in pairs or small groups on the Define It organizer. (Journal, p. 88)
- Have students add words to the Your Choice box and their personal word bank.
- Use the Show You Know exercise to assess students' understanding.

Model adding a word to the Word Bank by thinking aloud:

> **THINK ALOUD** *There were quite a few words in this article that I would like to put in a personal word bank. Message is one of them. I hear that all the time. People talk about leaving a message on voicemail or text messaging someone, or they say, "Would you give a message to someone for me?"*

UNIT 3

The Price of Discovery

PROGRAM RESOURCES

ANTHOLOGY pp. 96–99

TEACHING GUIDE AND RESOURCES
- Opinion and Reasons Organizer **p. 148**
- Answer Key **p. 121**

REAL WORLD WRITING JOURNAL pp. 90–93

ANTHOLOGY

Preteach

Activate Prior Knowledge Take a poll for each invention in the Real-Life Connection. Students will revisit answers after they read.

Build Background *A space shuttle flight can cost up to $1 billion. Some other things that also cost $1 billion are: 400 30-second Super Bowl commercials, 8 F-35 fighter planes, and the 2004 presidential campaign.*

Introduce Vocabulary

- Read aloud the sentences from the article in which boldface vocabulary words appear. Discuss what each word means in context.
- Give students the opportunity to practice the vocabulary words in a new context. Work with students to create new sentences for each term.
- *Build Academic Vocabulary* Talk with students about how you might *explore* and *examine* when you *investigate* something. Encourage volunteers to give examples.

Teach

Focus on the Big Question Ask the Article BQ, "Is the information we gain from space exploration worth the cost?" Students will answer this question after reading.

- *Connect to the Unit Big Question* Have students read the Unit BQ and Article BQ. Then ask students how we might measure the value of learning new information.

Preread the Article Before students read, have them read the Wrap It Up questions. Based on these questions, have them infer what the article will discuss. Model inferring for students:

THINK ALOUD *The questions are about a space shuttle, landing on the moon, the space program, and NASA. That tells me the article is about space and travel in space. One of the questions asks about whether it is costly. So, I know the article will talk about how much money is spent on space exploration.*

Model how to write a prediction about the article.

Conduct a Guided Reading Read the article to students as they follow along. Pause after each section to monitor students' comprehension.

- Ask "5 Ws and an H" questions.
- Have volunteers summarize the main idea of each section.

Reflect on the Article After reading the article, review ideas introduced before or during reading.

- Have students revisit the Real-Life Connection and check their prereading answers.
- Have students add to that list of inventions some of the other things the space program has given us.

Practice and Apply

Discuss the Questions Gauge students' comprehension and help them develop critical reading skills. (Answer Key, p. 121)

Connect to the Big Question Have students use the Opinion and Reasons organizer to answer the BQ.

- Have students write the Article BQ on their organizers. Tell students to begin by writing their opinion about the cost of the space program.
- Tell students to write reasons that support their opinions, using the article as a source.
- Call on volunteers to answer the BQ. Ask students to support their opinions with reasons based on the article and from their organizers.

Assess

Use this informal assessment before moving on to the Writing Journal activities. Have students create a space program fact sheet. Divide the class into groups and assign each group one section of the article. Tell them to choose two to five important facts from their section. Bring the class back together and combine the reports from each group to make a fact sheet.

Reach All Learners

Build Fluency Choose a section from the article for a Paired Reading.

- Pair students and have them read silently.
- Direct one student to read aloud while the other follows along making notes.
- The listener provides suggestions and feedback. Students then reverse roles.

Use Small Groups Have students create a press conference interview with a NASA official. Divide the class into small groups to discuss what questions should be asked. Each group should make a list of at least two questions. Have a volunteer from each group be a journalist in the press conference, armed with his or her group's questions. Ask one student to take the role of the NASA official, or take that role yourself and hold the press conference.

Assist Students Having Difficulty If students have difficulty writing notes, remind them that they do not need to use complete sentences.

- Work with students to make a list of abbreviations to use when taking notes. Write the abbreviations on the board.
- Model for students examples of taking notes for different activities in the lesson.

WRITING JOURNAL

Extend

Write About It Students will write speeches expressing opinions about the cost of the space program.

- Read and discuss the Writing Prompt. (Journal, p. 90) Review the Writing Rubric.
- Encourage students to add more points to the rubric to guide their work.
- Model how to use the organizer.
- Students should use the Check It and Fix It Section and Writing Checklist to revise and evaluate their work.

Teaching Tip Working on a speech is an excellent opportunity to build fluency. Have students pair up to read each other's speeches. Then ask for volunteers to present their own or a classmate's speech to the class.

Vocabulary Workshop Students extend their thinking about Word Bank words.

- Students work in pairs or small groups on the Define It organizer. (Journal, p. 92)
- Have students add words to the Your Choice box and their personal word bank.
- Use the Show You Know exercise to assess students' understanding.

Model spelling words with word endings by thinking aloud:

> **THINK ALOUD** *I see how adding* -ation *to* explore *makes* exploration. *What happened to the* e *at the end of* explore? *I dropped it. Do I always drop the final* e? *The next word is* imagine. *That becomes* imagination. *The* e *was dropped again.*

Someone Has to Do It

PROGRAM RESOURCES

ANTHOLOGY pp. 100–103

TEACHING GUIDE AND RESOURCES
- Word Pyramid **p. 157**
- Two-Column Journal **p. 153**
- Answer Key **p. 122**

REAL WORLD WRITING JOURNAL pp. 94–97

ANTHOLOGY

Preteach

Activate Prior Knowledge Take a poll of *true* or *false* for each statement in the Real-Life Connection. Students will revisit answers after they read.

Build Background *Adults are not the only ones with dangerous jobs. Teens also have to take precautions. The five most dangerous jobs for teens are: working in agriculture, late-night retail, construction in high places, forklift and tractor driving, and street corner or door-to-door sales.*

Introduce Vocabulary

- Have students work in pairs to read the Word Bank words and definitions to each other. Then have each pair find the boldface words in the selection.
- Help students fill out the Word Pyramid for each word.
- *Build Academic Vocabulary* Write the academic vocabulary words on the board. Have students write sentences using the words to describe an archeological discovery.

Teach

Focus on the Big Question Ask the Article BQ, "What can we learn from people who do dangerous jobs?" Students will answer this question after reading.

- *Connect to the Unit Big Question* Have students reread the Unit BQ. Ask students whether they think the BQ is talking about factual information or life lessons.

Preread the Article Before students read, model how to preview and predict:

THINK ALOUD *This article has a photo and a chart. I use graphic features to make a prediction about the article. The photo shows a ship at sea. The chart shows the ten most dangerous jobs in the United States. I think this article will be about some of the dangers workers encounter on jobs at sea.*

Ask students to write a prediction.

Conduct a Guided Reading Read the article to the students as they follow along. Pause after each section to monitor students' comprehension.

- After each section, ask a volunteer to summarize what he or she has just read.
- Have students make connections between the text and the world as they read.

Reflect on the Article After reading the article, review ideas introduced before or during reading.

- Retake the poll from the Real-Life Connection. Have answers changed? Ask students why.
- Have students reread their predictions and discuss their accuracy. What have they learned that is different from their predictions?

Practice and Apply

Discuss the Questions Gauge students' comprehension and help them develop critical reading skills. (Answer Key, p. 122)

Connect to the Big Question Have students use the Two-Column Journal to answer the BQ.

- Have students write the Article BQ on their organizers. Then talk about reasons people do the dangerous jobs in the article. Have students list these in the chart.
- Then have students answer the BQ in the "My Thoughts" column.
- Invite volunteers to share their answers with the class.

Assess

Use this informal assessment before moving on to the Writing Journal activities. Have students explore the classroom, looking for things that may have been produced in part by people doing dangerous jobs. Each student should write down at least three things. Then, ask students to share their lists with the class. Discuss what part a dangerous job might have played in producing or transporting books, computers, chairs, and so forth.

Reach All Learners

Build Fluency Use the first section of the article to do a "preview of coming attractions."

- Divide the class into small groups. Each group should choose one or two students to do the actual reading.
- The rest of each group will "produce" the preview. They may use drawings, music, or any other visual or auditory aids.
- The group should also "direct" the actors, helping them to read with expression.
- Have the groups present their previews.

Use Small Groups Use a Write-Around activity to answer the first Use Clues question.

- In groups of four, have each student begin with a piece of paper with the Article BQ written across the top.
- Have students write a response for one minute and then pass their papers to the right. The one-minute writing begins again, and students add to the paper in front of them.
- Continue until all four students have written on each paper. Share writing in a class discussion.

Assist Students Having Difficulty If students struggle to use vocabulary words in new context, allow them to work with a partner.

- Have students complete the Draw-Define-Use Organizer with a partner.
- Provide dictionaries for support. Allow students to look up meanings of new words before writing their own definitions.

WRITING JOURNAL

Extend

Write About It Students will write a handout defining dirty jobs.

- Read and discuss the Writing Prompt. (Journal, p. 94) Review the Writing Rubric.
- Encourage students to add more points to the rubric to guide their work.
- Model how to use the organizer.
- Students should use the Check It and Fix It Section and Writing Checklist to revise and evaluate their work.

Model how to organize thoughts by thinking aloud:

> **THINK ALOUD** *I need to talk about what a dangerous job is. I know I will want to give some examples. I should check the article for examples. And I will be sure to write some good things about some of these jobs to present a balanced viewpoint.*

Vocabulary Workshop Students extend their thinking about Word Bank words.

- Students work in pairs or small groups on the Define It organizer. (Journal, p. 96)
- Have students add words to the Your Choice box and their personal word bank.
- Use the Show You Know exercise to assess students' understanding.

Teaching Tip Give students considerable latitude in their definitions on the Define It graphic organizer. Any phrase that indicates an understanding of the word is acceptable.

Have No Fear

PROGRAM RESOURCES

ANTHOLOGY pp. 104–107

TEACHING GUIDE AND RESOURCES
- Problem and Solution Map **p. 149**
- Main Idea Map **p. 146**
- Answer Key **p. 122**

REAL WORLD WRITING JOURNAL pp. 98–101

ANTHOLOGY

Preteach

Activate Prior Knowledge Draw the Real-Life Connection chart on the board. Take a poll of students' fears and add results to the chart. Students will revisit answers after they read.

Build Background *About one in ten people in the United States suffers from a phobia, a fear that is not connected to an actual danger. Almost one in twenty has a phobia that seriously affects his or her life.*

Introduce Vocabulary

- Have student pairs take turns reading the words and definitions in the Word Bank.
- Ask each pair to choose two words from the word bank and list synonyms for each word. Encourage students to use a dictionary or thesaurus to find synonyms. Have students write a sentence using the vocabulary word and another using its synonym. Invite volunteers to share their sentences with the class.
- *Build Academic Vocabulary* Point out the academic vocabulary in the Word Bank. Ask volunteers to tell whether the words would most likely be used in a social studies assignment, a book report, or a math book. Have the students explain their answers.

Teach

Focus on the Big Question Ask the Article BQ, "How can people learn to overcome phobias?" Students will answer this question after reading.

- *Connect to the Unit Big Question* Read the Unit and Article BQs aloud. Make sure students understand the word *phobias*. Ask students if a phobia is always unreasonable.

Preread the Article Before students read, model how to preview the article and ask questions about it:

> **THINK ALOUD** *The title of this article is "Have No Fear." I wonder what that means. Everyone is afraid sometimes, so I think it does not mean "absolutely no fear." So I have a question to answer as I read: Is there a way to get rid of some of our fears? I think the article will help me answer that question.*

Ask students to write questions about the article.

Conduct a Guided Reading Read the article to the students as they follow along. Pause after each section to monitor students' comprehension.

- Have students make connections to their personal experience.
- Ask students to make an inference about how phobias may have helped humans survive.

Reflect on the Article After reading the article, review ideas introduced before or during reading.

- Have students reread their responses to the Real-Life Connection.
- Have students discuss whether they have found answers to their prereading questions.

Practice and Apply

Discuss the Questions Gauge students' comprehension and help them develop critical reading skills. (Answer Key, p. 122)

Connect to the Big Question Have students use the Problem and Solution Map to answer the BQ.

- Have students write the Article BQ on their organizers. Model writing the problem: *Kim is afraid of spiders.*
- Tell students to refer to the article and write the solution and Kim's response to it on the graphic organizer.
- Discuss how people can overcome phobias.

Assess

Have students write a short summary of the article. To prepare, have students use the Main Idea Map to write the main idea of the article and supporting ideas. Remind them that a good summary includes only the most important ideas.

Reach All Learners

Build Fluency Choose a section from the article and have students do a class reading to practice fluency.

- Have students read the section in pairs and coach each other on fluency. Tell students that they may call on you for help or advice.
- Then have each student read one or two lines from the section aloud to the entire class.

Use Small Groups Have students create "Have No Fear" posters.

- Provide small groups of students with art materials to create a poster.
- Have groups discuss the article and choose one tip for dealing with fear to illustrate.
- Have students include a slogan-like caption with their poster.
- Display posters around the classroom.

Assist Students Having Difficulty If students struggle to find subjects for their Show You Know cartoons, brainstorm subjects as a class. You might also allow students to clip actual comic strips from newspapers or other sources and then rewrite the words that you have cut out of the speech bubbles.

WRITING JOURNAL

Extend

Write About It Students will write a letter to a student that gives advice about overcoming fears.

- Read and discuss the Writing Prompt. (Journal, p. 98) Review the Writing Rubric.
- Encourage students to add more points to the rubric to guide their work.
- Students should use the Check It and Fix It Section and Writing Checklist to revise and evaluate their work.

Teaching Tip To help students decide what advice they want to give, go through the article together as a class and spot sentences that tell what to do about phobias.

Vocabulary Workshop Students extend their thinking about Word Bank words.

- Students work in pairs or small groups on the Define It organizer. (Journal, p. 100)
- Have students add words to the Your Choice box and their personal word bank.
- Use the Show You Know exercise to assess students' understanding.

Model brainstorming for the comic strip by thinking aloud:

> **THINK ALOUD** *I think I will look at all the words and see if anything comes to mind. Maybe I will write about a science fair. I think I want two characters so they can talk to each other. I will draw them in the first box. One of them will say, "What was your approach to your project?"*

What should we learn?

Introduce the Unit Project

Poster Students will create a poster presenting an answer to the Big Question: *What should we learn?*

- Read through the steps of the assignment with students.
- Point out the rubric so that students will know their goals for the assignment. Add other rubric points with students to guide their work.
- Allow time for students to organize and illustrate their presentation. Encourage listeners to offer their feedback and advice on the presentation.

Model Model how to collect items to display on a poster:

> **THINK ALOUD** *I have chosen "The Price of Discovery" as one of my articles. I could use a picture of the space shuttle, but I really want to show how we have benefited from the space program. I think I will find pictures of some of the things we use today that came from the space program. There are so many of them that I am sure I can find some in just about any magazine.*

Teaching Tip When doing visual arts projects, it is important to make achievement accessible to students who cannot paint or draw. Have available for these students magazines from which to cut images and, if possible, a way to generate readable text, such as a computer with a word processing program and a printer or a typewriter.

Conclude the Unit

Review Unit Objectives Return to the unit objectives and ask students to evaluate how well they mastered each one on a scale of 1 to 5, with 1 being low and 5 being high. Discuss how lower scores could be improved.

Reflect on the Learning Examine the bulletin board with students. Ask them to reflect on what they have learned. They can write or discuss with the whole class or in small groups. Prompt students' thinking with questions such as:

- What was the most interesting article you read? What did you like about it?
- How did your ideas about learning change?
- Which topic would you like to know more about?
- How did the writing assignments and the poster help you form your ideas about learning?
- What other article topics do you think could be included in this unit? How would those topics help people form ideas about learning?

Name _____

Word Bank Quiz

WORD LIST A			
analyze	curiosity	examine	organize
approach	discipline	experiment	possible
background	discover	information	understand

Ten of the unit Word Bank words are defined in parentheses in the article below. As you read the article, use Word List A, above, to figure out which word best fits each definition. Write the word on the line provided. (You will not use every word on the list.) Then go on to the next page of the quiz.

The Science of Discovery

Scientists work to (**1. know the meaning of**) _____ the world around them. They use many different methods to (**2. find**) _____ the truth about plants and animals, weather, oceans, and outer space. One scientist may (**3. look very carefully at**) _____ a single petal on a rose, while another may (**4. divide into parts to see how they fit**) _____ something as large and complicated as a rainforest. Other scientists may spend years gathering (**5. the facts about**) _____ about something in nature simply by watching. Some scientists use a very different (**6. organized way to do something**) _____.

Still, all scientists have certain things in common. It does not matter what (**7. experience, knowledge, and education**) _____ a scientist has or what country or way of life he or she comes from. It does not matter what (**8. subject or field of study**) _____ he or she works in. All scientists have a deep (**9. interest in learning**) _____ about some part of the natural world that leads them to study and research. As they gather and (**10. use a system to put in order**) _____ their data, they follow the rules of science.

WORD LIST B			
curiosity	facts	investigate	question
evaluate	inquire	organize	recall
explore	interview	possible	topic

Ten more Word Bank words are defined in parentheses in the article below.
As you read the article, use Word List B, above, to figure out which word
best fits each definition. Write the word on the line provided. (You will not
use every word on the list.)

Writing a Research Paper

Writing a research paper is not difficult if you take it step by step. First, choose a

(11. a subject or general idea) _____ for your paper, the one

main thing it will be about. To do that, you may want to **(12. look around or over)**

_____ the Internet or the library. Then, gather your

(13. information that can be shown to be true) _____.

Several methods are **(14. able to happen or be done)** _____

at this stage. You will probably **(15. find information about in order to understand)**

_____ your topic in a number of sources, such as books and articles.

If you go to the librarian and **(16. ask questions)** _____ about

these sources, he or she will help you **(17. form an opinion based on knowledge)**

_____ them to decide which ones are most reliable. You might also

do an **(18. series of questions one person asks another)** _____ with

an expert to find answers for your paper. You can use a tape recorder or make notes to

help you **(19. remember)** _____ what the expert tells you.

Finally, you will want to **(20. challenge the truth of)** _____

everything you have learned. Do not just accept what people tell you. Draw your own

conclusions and form your own opinions.

UNIT 4

What is the best way to communicate?

Unit Overview

The articles in this unit explore the topic of communication. Students will read articles about specific forms of communication as well as articles about how people's actions and behaviors communicate their thoughts, beliefs, and feelings. As students read they will evaluate how people communicate and what works best.

Launch the Unit

Connect to the Big Question Read the introduction with students and examine the illustration. Ask questions such as:

- *What are some different ways people communicate with one another?*
- *How are the people in the illustration communicating?*
- *How are these methods of communication good ones? What problems might be caused by both forms?*
- *What methods do you use to communicate with friends or family?*

Use the prompt on the page as the basis for journal writing or for small group or whole class discussion. Students can share their ideas with partners or in small groups.

Anchor Students' Thinking Start a bulletin board on which you post the Big Question. Throughout the unit, students can add to the bulletin board. Use ideas such as the following:

- Have students post their thoughts on the types of communication described in the articles.
- Keep a list on the bulletin board of ways people communicate. Have students add ideas to the list and note which they personally have used.
- Encourage students to add articles about communication from newspapers, magazines, and the Internet to the bulletin board. Have them write brief evaluations of each way to communicate.
- Ask students to contribute examples of communication and miscommunication from their own lives or from news reports. Have students connect these accounts to the Big Question.

Unit Objectives

Share these objectives with students. As you read the articles in this unit, you will:

- Identify different ways that people communicate.
- Determine an answer to the Big Question: *What is the best way to communicate?* Explain your answer using details from the articles and from your own experiences.
- Use vocabulary words to talk and write about communication.
- Form an opinion for a TV commercial and support that opinion with reasons.

UNIT 4

Thinking of You

PROGRAM RESOURCES

ANTHOLOGY pp. 112–115

TEACHING GUIDE AND RESOURCES
- Venn Diagram **p. 154**
- Answer Key **p. 124**

REAL WORLD WRITING JOURNAL pp. 104–107

ANTHOLOGY

Preteach

Activate Prior Knowledge Survey students about whether they agree with each statement in the Real-Life Connection. Students will revisit answers after they read.

Build Background *Americans spend about $7.5 billion a year on greeting cards, with the average person receiving about twenty cards per year. Which times of year do you think most people give and receive cards?*

Introduce Vocabulary

- Write the Word Bank words and the definitions in random order in two columns on the board. Have students match each word to its definition.
- Work with students to create a sentence for each word.
- *Build Academic Vocabulary* Ask how students might use academic vocabulary words in other classes. *Produce* and *translate*, for example, might be used in a social studies class. Ask students to write sentences using the words.

Teach

Focus on the Big Question Ask the Article BQ, "Are greeting cards a good way to communicate feelings?" Students will answer this question after reading.

- *Connect to the Unit Big Question* Write the Unit and Article BQs on the board. Circle the word *communicate* in each. Ask students to name different ways people communicate to link the BQs.

Preread the Article Before students read, model how to preview and predict:

> **THINK ALOUD** *You can quickly read, or skim, the article to get an idea of what you are going to read about. By looking at the title, pictures, captions, and subtitles, I predict this article will be about the history of greeting cards and how they have changed over time.*

Students can make predictions of their own.

Conduct a Guided Reading Read the article to students as they follow along. Pause after each section to monitor students' comprehension.

- Remind students to ask questions and look for answers as they read.
- Ask a volunteer to summarize the section.

Reflect on the Article After reading the article, review ideas introduced before or during reading.

- Survey students on the Real-Life Connection questions again. Have answers changed? Ask students why.
- Ask students whether they made changes to their predictions. Have them explain why or why not.

Practice and Apply

Discuss the Questions Gauge students' comprehension and help them develop critical reading skills. (Answer Key, p. 124)

Connect to the Big Question Use a Venn Diagram to have students answer the BQ.

- Have students write the Article BQ on their diagrams. Have them label the circles "greeting cards" and "face-to-face."
- Ask volunteers to describe how communicating with greeting cards and face-to-face is similar and different. Model writing student suggestions in the appropriate sections of the diagram.
- Have students use their diagrams to answer the BQ.

Assess

For an informal assessment, have students work in groups to describe each of the following:

- cards from the 1400s
- cards during World War II
- cards during the 1950s
- cards during the 1980s
- cards during the 1990s

Have students use this information to write a short summary of how communication through cards has changed over time.

Reach All Learners

Build Fluency Choose two sections with multiple punctuation marks (commas, periods, quotation marks) and instruct pairs to practice fluency with correct punctuation.

- Pair students and have each student read a different section silently.
- Have one student read aloud while the other listens. Have the student who listens say what punctuation he or she heard and provide feedback to the reader.
- Have students reverse roles.

Use Small Groups Use a group activity to have students respond to the Article BQ.

- In groups of four, have students create one of the types of cards from the Assess section.
- Have students compare their completed card to other ways of communicating the same emotion (face-to-face, phone call, handwritten note, e-mail message, and so on).
- Discuss how the cards compare to other ways of communicating.

Assist Students Having Difficulty If students have a hard time comparing greeting cards to other forms of communication, help them list features.

- Ask students to provide details about communicating with greeting cards.
- Then have students provide details about another form of communication.
- Model adding these details to the Venn Diagram, pointing out that similarities belong in the center section.

WRITING JOURNAL

Extend

Write About It Students will use a Three-Column Chart and write a paragraph explaining the best form of communication.

- Read and discuss the Writing Prompt. (Journal, p. 104) Review the Writing Rubric.
- Encourage students to add more points to the rubric to guide their work.
- Model how to use the organizer.
- Students should use the Check It and Fix It and the Writing Checklist to revise and evaluate their work.

Model planning for writing by thinking aloud:

THINK ALOUD *I want to be sure that I can support my explanation about which kind of apology would be best. After I fill out the chart, I will look at which form of communication has the most pros. This will be the strongest explanation. These pros will help support my explanation.*

Vocabulary Workshop Students extend their thinking about Word Bank words.

- Students work in pairs or small groups on the Define It organizer. (Journal, p. 106)
- Have students add words to the Your Choice box and their personal word bank.
- Use the Show You Know exercise to assess students' understanding.

Teaching Tip Have the class list possible responses to the All in the Family exercise. Have students explain how the spelling and meaning change with each suffix. Ask a volunteer to copy responses on a large piece of paper or poster board. Post the responses on a classroom bulletin board so that students can refer to the word families often.

Word on the Wire

PROGRAM RESOURCES

ANTHOLOGY pp. 116–119

TEACHING GUIDE AND RESOURCES
- K-W-L Chart **p. 145**
- Answer Key **p. 124**

REAL WORLD WRITING JOURNAL pp. 108–111

ANTHOLOGY

Preteach

Activate Prior Knowledge Have students individually copy and complete the chart in the Real-Life Connection. Students will revisit answers after they read.

Build Background *Most schools have rules about students having cell phones. In 2008, for example, the Austin, Texas, school district allowed students in all grades, including elementary, to have cell phones in school. In New York City schools, students can bring phones to school but may not have them in class.*

Introduce Vocabulary

- Read through the Word Bank words and definitions with students.
- Have students use gestures or drawings to demonstrate the meaning of the verbs.
- *Build Academic Vocabulary* Write the academic vocabulary words on the board. Discuss with students how they might use *communicate*, *technology*, and *transmit* in other subject areas.

Teach

Focus on the Big Question Ask the Article BQ, "Do cell phones belong in school?" Students will answer this question after reading.

- *Connect to the Unit Big Question* Write the Unit and Article BQs on the board. Ask students how cell phones help or hurt people's ability to communicate.

Preread the Article Give students copies of the K-W-L Chart. Model how to use it:

> **THINK ALOUD** *In the first column, I write what I know about cell phones in schools. I know that many, but not all, students have cell phones, so I write*

that in the first column. I want to find out how cell phones can be used in a good way in school, so I write that in the second column.

Tell students they will fill out the third column as they read the article.

Conduct a Guided Reading Read the article to students as they follow along. Pause after each section to monitor students' comprehension.

- Ask students what they have learned about cell phones in schools. Have them add the information to the third column of their organizer.
- Ask students whether they agree with what they are reading.

Reflect on the Article After reading the article, review ideas introduced before or during reading.

- Have students look at their charts from the Real-Life Connection. After reading the article, what would they add to the chart?
- Have students look at their completed K-W-L Charts. Did they find out everything they wanted to learn? After reading, what else do they wonder about?

Practice and Apply

Discuss the Questions Gauge students' comprehension and help them develop critical reading skills. (Answer Key, p. 124)

Connect to the Big Question Refocus students' attention on the Article BQ.

- Have students write a response to the Article BQ. Provide a list of options, such as *never*, *in some situations*, and *always* that students can use in their response.
- Call for volunteers to share their responses.

Assess

Have students write their own assessments.

- Each student should write two multiple-choice and two short-answer test questions on a blank sheet of paper. Have students create answer keys for their tests.
- Have student pairs exchange and take each other's tests. Have students score and discuss the results.

Reach All Learners

Build Fluency Choose a section from the article to model reading in phrases and conveying meaning.

- Read one sentence at a time, emphasizing natural phrasing and meaning.
- Have students follow along as you read.
- Then have students chorally repeat the sentence following your emphasis.

Use Small Groups Have students work in groups to debate the Article BQ.

- Organize students into groups of three or four. Have each group choose to argue for or against students having cell phones in school. The group works together to create arguments.
- Have groups with opposing views debate the issue. Each student should participate in the debate.

Assist Students Having Difficulty If students struggle to find main ideas and details in the article, provide them with an outline for taking notes.

- The outline should include the article title and any subheads with space for notes.
- Allow time after reading the article to go over the outline using an overhead transparency.
- Have students compare the information on the outline with the third column of their K-W-L Charts.

WRITING JOURNAL

Extend

Write About It Students will use a T-Chart and write a student's guide to responsible cell phone use.

- Read and discuss the Writing Prompt. (Journal, p. 108) Review the Writing Rubric.
- Encourage students to add more points to the rubric to guide their work.
- Model how to use the organizer.
- Students should use the Check It and Fix It and the Writing Checklist to revise and evaluate their work.

Teaching Tip Discuss with students the importance of thinking about their audience for the guide: other students. As a class, brainstorm ideas about how students are most likely to use their cell phones and how this is different from how adults use their cell phones.

Vocabulary Workshop Students extend their thinking about Word Bank words.

- Students work in pairs or small groups on the Define It organizer. (Journal, p. 110)
- Have students add words to the Your Choice box and their personal word bank.
- Use the Show You Know exercise to assess students' understanding.

As you write, model by thinking aloud:

> **THINK ALOUD** *While I was reading the article, I noticed the word* interfere *on page 117. I have seen that word used a lot, like in football when there is pass interference or when people talk about something interfering with their cell phone or TV signal. I am going to add it to the Your Choice list and my personal word bank so that I can use it correctly.*

UNIT 4

A Show of Strength

PROGRAM RESOURCES

ANTHOLOGY pp. 120–123

TEACHING GUIDE AND RESOURCES
- Guess It and Check It Chart **p. 143**
- Main Idea Map **p. 146**
- Answer Key **p. 124**

REAL WORLD WRITING JOURNAL pp. 112–115

ANTHOLOGY

Preteach

Activate Prior Knowledge Have students copy the web from the Real-Life Connection. Students will revisit answers after they read.

> **THINK ALOUD** *I use this web before I read to begin thinking about heroes. When I hear hero, I think about people who risk their own safety to help others. I write "help others" in one of the outer circles. I add specific heroes, like firefighters, to other circles.*

Have students complete their webs, adding additional circles if necessary.

Build Background *Have you ever been scared or in an intense situation where you needed to act quickly? If so, you probably felt the results of adrenaline. Adrenaline is a hormone your body produces to help you act quickly in a dangerous or exciting situation.*

Introduce Vocabulary
- Have student pairs use the Guess It and Check It Chart. Have them write the Word Bank words in the first column.
- Ask students to find the boldface words in the article and write clues they found about the words' meanings. Students should guess the meaning, then check their guess using the Word Bank.
- *Build Academic Vocabulary* All the words in the Word Bank are academic vocabulary. Have students explain how they use the words in other classes.

Teach

Focus on the Big Question Ask the Article BQ, "How do real-life heroes show courage?" Students will answer this question after reading.

- *Connect to the Unit Big Question* Write the Unit and Article BQs on the board. Ask students what heroes might communicate when they help others.

Preread the Article Before students read, have them preview and predict.
- Point out the title, subheadings, and photograph captions and read them aloud.
- Ask students to use the features to write a prediction about what the article will discuss.

Conduct a Guided Reading Read the article to students as they follow along. Pause after each section to monitor students' comprehension.
- Ask questions about each section, such as *Who is the section about? What did the person do?* and *Where did it happen?*
- Call on a volunteer to summarize each section.

Reflect on the Article After reading the article, review ideas introduced before or during reading.
- Have students revisit their webs from the Real-Life Connection. Ask them to add information after reading the article.
- Ask students how the three heroes were similar or different.

Practice and Apply

Discuss the Questions Gauge students' comprehension and help them develop critical reading skills. (Answer Key, p. 124)

Connect to the Big Question Have students use the Main Idea Map to answer the BQ.
- Have students write the Article BQ on their organizers. Have them complete an outer section for each of the three hero stories.
- Have students use the center section to make an observation about all three real-life heroes.

Assess

Play a matching game with students to informally assess their understanding.

- Divide students into three groups and assign each one of the heroes.
- Have students write short clues about their hero on separate index cards. Collect cards.
- Have students create a three-column chart, a column for each hero. Read each clue and have students write the clue in the correct column.
- As a class, review answers. Have students locate the clues in the article.

Reach All Learners

Build Fluency Choose sections from the article for Radio Reads.

- Model reading a section as if you are delivering a radio or TV news report.
- Assign each student a section and have students practice reading silently first. Explain that they should practice reading as if they will be reading a news story on the radio or on TV.
- Have volunteers read their section to the class.

Use Small Groups Have students write an interview with one of the heroes.

- Have groups of four choose one of the heroes.
- Have students write an interview with the person that explores what happened and why the hero did what he or she did. Students may use quotations from the article and create their own.
- Have two volunteers from each group perform their interview for the class.

Assist Students Having Difficulty If students have difficulty writing an interview, explain the purpose of an interview.

- Explain that an interview usually starts with asking about facts. Model asking "5 Ws and an H" questions.
- Tell students that after an interviewer asks about facts, he or she usually asks deeper questions that cannot be answered with "yes" or "no." Provide examples, such as *If this happened again, what would you do differently?* and *How did this event change your life?*

WRITING JOURNAL

Extend

Write About It Students will use a graphic organizer and write a feature article on a hero for their school newspaper.

- Read and discuss the Writing Prompt. (Journal, p. 112) Review the Writing Rubric.
- Encourage students to add more points to the rubric to guide their work.
- Model how to use the organizer.
- Students should use the Check It and Fix It and the Writing Checklist to revise and evaluate their work.

Model your prewriting process by thinking aloud:

> **THINK ALOUD** *The article talks about three heroes, but I am supposed to write about just one. Since I have to write a news article on this person, I want to pick the one I think is the most amazing. That way, my article will be more convincing. I will look at the notes I made and use those to help me choose a focus.*

Vocabulary Workshop Students extend their thinking about Word Bank words.

- Students work in pairs or small groups on the Define It organizer. (Journal, p. 114)
- Have students add words to the Your Choice box and their personal word bank.
- Use the Show You Know exercise to assess students' understanding.

Teaching Tip Have the class brainstorm words that begin with the prefix *re-*. Create a poster with the prefix and its definition at the top. Add the *re-* words generated by students.

The Big Money

PROGRAM RESOURCES

ANTHOLOGY pp. 124–127

TEACHING GUIDE AND RESOURCES
- Two-Column Journal p. 153
- Answer Key p. 125

REAL WORLD WRITING JOURNAL pp. 116–119

ANTHOLOGY

Preteach

Activate Prior Knowledge Take a poll for each statement in the Real-Life Connection. Students will revisit answers after they read.

Build Background *According to the U.S. government, the more education people have, the more money they make. Adults without high school diplomas make about one third less than those with high school diplomas. People with a four-year college degree on average make more than twice as much as people without a high school diploma.*

Introduce Vocabulary

- Read aloud the sentences from the article in which boldface vocabulary words appear. Discuss the context clues in the sentences that help students figure out each word's meaning.
- Have students practice using the words in a different context.
- *Build Academic Vocabulary* Ask how students might use the words *media* and *transmit* in a social studies class.

Teach

Focus on the Big Question Ask the Article BQ, "What message do we send with the salaries we pay to 'stars'?" Students will answer this question after reading.

- *Connect to the Unit Big Question* Write the Unit and Article BQs on the board. Elaborate on any difficult words.

Preread the Article Before students read, have them preview the title and first and last paragraphs and make predictions about content.

- Read aloud the title.
- Have students read the first and last paragraphs. Ask volunteers to summarize each.
- Have students use the title and first and last paragraphs to write a prediction.

Conduct a Guided Reading Read the article to students as they follow along. Pause after each section to monitor students' comprehension. Model finding the main idea of a section:

> **THINK ALOUD** *In the article's first section, there is information about how much money different stars make. The article mentions Tiger Woods and Oprah Winfrey. Those are important details, but not the main idea. The main idea is that there are different kinds of stars, they are the best at what they do; and they are paid a lot of money.*

- Call on volunteers to provide a main idea for each section.
- Ask other students to provide details that support the main ideas.

Reflect on the Article After reading the article, review ideas introduced before or during reading.

- Tally students' responses to the Real-Life Connection statements. Have answers changed? Ask students why.
- Ask students how their predictions were similar to and different from the actual article. Have them explain the similarities and differences.

Practice and Apply

Discuss the Questions Gauge student's comprehension and help them develop critical reading skills. (Answer Key, p. 125)

Connect to the Big Question Students use the Two-Column Journal to respond.

- Have students write the Article BQ on their organizers. Instruct students to write observations about salaries in one column and their thoughts in the other.
- Ask students to use their thoughts from their organizers to help them answer the question.

Assess

Have students create a Learning Log for you to informally assess. Students should answer these questions:

- What did you learn in class today?
- What did you think was interesting?
- What questions do you still have?

Reach All Learners

Build Fluency Choose a section from the article for a Paired Reading.

- Pair students and have them read silently.
- Direct one student to read the paragraph aloud while the other follows, making notes.
- The listener provides suggestions and feedback. Students then reverse roles.

Use Small Groups Engage students with a Write-Around activity.

- In groups of four, have each student begin with a piece of paper with the Article BQ written across the top.
- Have students write a response for one minute and then pass their papers to the right. The one-minute writing begins again, and students add to the paper in front of them.
- Continue until all four students have written on each paper. Discuss responses with the class.

Assist Students Having Difficulty If students struggle to monitor understanding, provide them with a note-taking strategy.

- Provide students with small- and medium-size sticky notes.
- Direct them to use the small sticky notes to mark important details, and the medium notes to write a main idea of each section.

WRITING JOURNAL

Extend

Write About It Students will use an Opinion and Reasons Organizer and write a letter to the editor of the local newspaper.

- Read and discuss the Writing Prompt. (Journal, p. 116) Review the Writing Rubric.
- Encourage students to add more points to the rubric to guide their work.
- Model how to use the organizer.
- Students should use the Check It and Fix It and the Writing Checklist to revise and evaluate their work.

Teaching Tip Explain to students that a letter to the editor of a newspaper usually expresses an opinion about something of interest to the community. It is different from a news story, which gives facts about something that happened.

Vocabulary Workshop Students extend their thinking about Word Bank words.

- Students work in pairs or small groups on the Define It organizer. (Journal, p. 118)
- Have students add words to the Your Choice box and their personal word bank.
- Use the Show You Know exercise to assess students' understanding.

Model completing the exercise by thinking aloud:

> **THINK ALOUD** *To solve these clue sentences, I am going to read the sentences carefully and circle any clues I see. The example sentence says the word is something that a magician or singer can do. I can tell from the word* do *that the term has to be an action word, or verb. Magicians or singers are people who perform. The Word Bank word must be* entertain.

UNIT 4

Pay Days

PROGRAM RESOURCES

ANTHOLOGY pp. 128–131

TEACHING GUIDE AND RESOURCES
- Word Pyramid **p. 157**
- Opinion and Reasons Organizer **p. 148**
- Answer Key **p. 125**

REAL WORLD WRITING JOURNAL pp. 120–123

ANTHOLOGY

Preteach

Activate Prior Knowledge Have students respond to the Real-Life Connection. Students will revisit answers after they read.

Build Background *The amount of money teens spend has increased rapidly in recent years, from $122 billion in 1999 to $169 billion in 2004. Teens spend 33 percent of their money on clothing and 21 percent on food.*

Introduce Vocabulary

- Have students work in pairs to read the Word Bank words and definitions to each other.
- Help students fill out the Word Pyramid for each word.

Model completing the organizer for *produce*:

> **THINK ALOUD** *I know a synonym is a word that means almost the same thing. Since produce means "to make" or "to create," I will add those to the second line. On the last line, I will write a sentence using the word.*

- *Build Academic Vocabulary* Have students work in pairs to write sentences explaining how *contribute* and *produce* could be used in social studies.

Teach

Focus on the Big Question Ask the Article BQ, "What do families communicate by paying kids an allowance?" Students will answer this question after reading.

- *Connect to the Unit Big Question* Write the Unit and Article BQs on the board. Pair students and have them discuss how the questions are similar.

Preread the Article Before students read, have them preview the article's features.

- Instruct students to read the title, subheadings, first sentence of each section, and bar graph.
- Ask students what information the bar graph provides.
- Have students work in pairs to write a sentence predicting what they will learn from the article.

Conduct a Guided Reading Read the article to students as they follow along. Pause after each section to monitor students' comprehension.

- Direct students to make connections between their own experiences and the information discussed in the article.
- Ask volunteers to share their connections with the class.

Reflect on the Article After reading the article, review ideas introduced before or during reading.

- Ask students if their ideas about whether teens should get an allowance have changed. Have them explain why.
- Ask students if their predictions were correct.

Practice and Apply

Discuss the Questions Gauge students' comprehension and help them develop critical reading skills. (Answer Key, p. 125)

Connect to the Big Question Use the Opinion and Reasons Organizer to have students answer the BQ.

- Have students write the Article BQ on their organizers. List some opinions that students could use to answer the question, such as *allowance teaches how to manage money, allowance is pay for chores, allowance is money for teens to use as they want.*
- Ask volunteers to share answers to the BQ and support opinions with reasons.

Assess

Informally assess students by having them write a dialogue between a teenager requesting an allowance and the teenager's parent.

- Instruct students that the teenager should use convincing reasons to persuade the parent to provide an allowance.
- Have students imagine how a parent would respond to the teen's arguments.
- Direct students to use information from the article in writing their dialogues.
- Invite volunteers to act out their dialogue.

Reach All Learners

Build Fluency Choose a section from the article for an Echo Read.

- Read the section aloud one sentence at a time, placing emphasis on expression and emotion.
- Have students chorally read each sentence after you, imitating your expression and intonation.

Use Small Groups Have students engage in active learning by writing a household guide and budget for a teenager's allowance.

- Have groups of three work together to create a guide or set of rules about allowances. Tell students to use ideas from the article.
- In their guides, students should establish a policy for how allowances are used in the household, such as how much money is given according to the teen's age, what the teen has to do in order to get the allowance, and how the allowance can be spent.
- Have groups share their guides with the class.

Assist Students Having Difficulty If students have difficulty with the assessment or small group activities, help them make personal connections.

- Ask students to think about what teenagers want and how their parents often view things differently.
- Have students explain why teens and adults might see the issue of allowances differently.

WRITING JOURNAL

Extend

Write About It Students will use the Opinion and Reasons Organizer and write a short TV report on allowances.

- Read and discuss the Writing Prompt. (Journal, p. 120) Review the Writing Rubric.
- Encourage students to add more points to the rubric to guide their work.
- Model how to use the organizer.
- Students should use the Check It and Fix It and the Writing Checklist to revise and evaluate their work.

Model drafting by thinking aloud:

THINK ALOUD *Since I am writing a TV report, I want to think about how to make my report interesting to people who are watching. The report will be read aloud, so I need to make sentences short, clear, and direct. If I include strong punctuation, such as question marks and exclamation points, I think that will help viewers understand my ideas better.*

Vocabulary Workshop Students extend their thinking about Word Bank words.

- Students work in pairs or small groups on the Define It organizer. (Journal, p. 122)
- Have students add words to the Your Choice box and their personal word bank.
- Use the Show You Know exercise to assess students' understanding.

Teaching Tip Point out to students that the Show You Know activity will be easier if they can think of topics that naturally include all the Word Bank words. Suggest that some topics, like school or team sports, make it easy to include words like *copy*, *learn*, and *contribute*.

UNIT 4

The Music Mix

PROGRAM RESOURCES

ANTHOLOGY pp. 132–135

TEACHING GUIDE AND RESOURCES
- Series of Events Map **p. 150**
- Venn Diagram **p. 154**
- Answer Key **p. 126**

REAL WORLD WRITING JOURNAL pp. 124–127

ANTHOLOGY

Preteach

Activate Prior Knowledge Have students complete the knowledge ratings in the Real-Life Connection. Students will revisit answers after they read.

Build Background *How people acquire and listen to music has changed over the last fifty years. In the 1950s, to get music people bought record albums in stores. Today, however, many people download, share, and listen to music using the Internet and portable devices like MP3 players and cell phones.*

Introduce Vocabulary

- Review the Word Bank words with students.
- Have students create sentences that include as many of the words as possible. Ask volunteers to share their sentences.
- *Build Academic Vocabulary* Talk with students about how *describe* and *reveal* are related. Have students use the words in a sentence.

Teach

Focus on the Big Question Ask the Article BQ, "When music takes different forms, does it send different messages?" Students will answer this question after reading.

- *Connect to the Unit Big Question* Write the Unit and Article BQs on the board. Have students work in pairs to discuss how the Article BQ can be used to help answer the Unit BQ.

Preread the Article Before students read, model how to preview and ask questions:

> **THINK ALOUD** *I am going to read the title first because it might give me a clue about the article. The title is "The Music Mix." I wonder what that means.*

> *I will look at the subheadings. I see the headings "Hip-Hop and Beyond" and "Stomp." I wonder if the article is about hip-hop, and I wonder what "Stomp" is. As I read, I will look for the answers to these questions.*

Model previewing the pictures and captions. Ask students to write questions they have about the article based on its features.

Conduct a Guided Reading Read the article to students as they follow along. Pause after each section to monitor students' comprehension.

- Work with students to find the main idea and supporting details for each section.
- Ask a volunteer to use the main ideas to summarize the section.

Reflect on the Article After reading the article, review ideas introduced before or during reading.

- Ask students what they learned about any of the types of music from the Real-Life Connection chart.
- Have students answer the questions they wrote while previewing the article.

Practice and Apply

Discuss the Questions Gauge students' comprehension and help them develop critical reading skills. (Answer Key, p. 126)

Connect to the Big Question Refocus students' attention on the Article BQ.

- Have students write the question on a piece of paper. Ask students to list different forms or types of music.
- Instruct students to think about the message sent by each type of music and jot down their thoughts.
- Have students use these notes to help them respond to the Article BQ.

Assess

To informally assess student learning, give them a copy of the Series of Events Map. Have students use the organizer to record the changes in music described in the article from the 1950s to today.

Reach All Learners

Build Fluency Choose a section from the article for a Paired Reading.

- Pair students and have them read silently.
- Direct one student to read aloud while the other follows along making notes.
- The listener provides suggestions and feedback. Students then reverse roles.

Use Small Groups Engage students in active learning by having them discuss the first Use Clues question.

- Have groups of three or four compare and contrast music from the 1950s and music today.
- Have students extend their thinking into how society today is different from the 1950s.
- Ask each group to share their thoughts with the class. Draw a Venn Diagram on the board and record responses.

Assist Students Having Difficulty If students struggle with comprehension, help them visualize and create images of ideas in the article.

- Model visualizing by using the salad comparison in the first paragraph.
- Work through the rest of the article asking students which senses they can use to help them understand the information.

WRITING JOURNAL

Extend

Write About It Students will use a T-Chart and write a proposal to their principal.

- Read and discuss the Writing Prompt. (Journal, p. 124) Review the Writing Rubric.
- Encourage students to add more points to the rubric to guide their work.
- Model how to use the organizer.
- Students should use the Check It and Fix It and the Writing Checklist to revise and evaluate their work.

Teaching Tip Before students work on the organizers, have a class discussion about what kind of music is appropriate or inappropriate for a school dance. Remind them that they will be making a suggestion to a principal and have them consider what a principal would find acceptable.

Vocabulary Workshop Students extend their thinking about Word Bank words.

- Students work in pairs or small groups on the Define It organizer. (Journal, p. 127)
- Have students add words to the Your Choice box and their personal word bank.
- Use the Show You Know exercise to assess students' understanding.

Model completing the exercise by thinking aloud:

> **THINK ALOUD** *To find a subject that I could use all these words with, I need to think about what they have in common. The Word Bank word* listen *is about hearing sounds, like music. I will try out the subject "music" with the other words and see if I can find a connection. If I do, I can write "music" as a topic in the center oval.*

UNIT 4

Follow Your Star

PROGRAM RESOURCES

ANTHOLOGY pp. 136–139

TEACHING GUIDE AND RESOURCES
- Making Personal Connections Organizer **p. 147**
- Answer Key **p. 126**

REAL WORLD WRITING JOURNAL pp. 128–131

ANTHOLOGY

Preteach

Activate Prior Knowledge Have students complete the chart in the Real-Life Connection. Students will revisit answers after they read.

Build Background *People get information about celebrities from different sources, such as TV shows, the Internet, and celebrity magazines. In recent years, sales of newspapers have decreased, but sales of celebrity and entertainment magazines continue to grow.*

Introduce Vocabulary

- Read aloud the sentences from the article in which boldface vocabulary words appear. Discuss each word's context.
- Work with students to create new sentences and use the words in different contexts.
- *Build Academic Vocabulary* Write the academic vocabulary words on the board. Have student pairs choose two words each. Ask each pair to write a sentence or two using the words to tell about something they learned in another class.

Teach

Focus on the Big Question Ask the Article BQ, "What does people's fascination with celebrity life communicate?" Students will answer this question after reading.

- *Connect to the Unit Big Question* Write the Unit and Article BQs on the board. Point out the word *communicate* in both questions. Ask students to explain how the word's meaning might be the same or different in the two questions.

Preread the Article Before students read, have them preview the article and make predictions about content. Model by thinking aloud:

THINK ALOUD *The title of this article is "Follow Your Star." I wonder what that means. Will the article be about the stars we see at night or people that are stars? By reading the first paragraph I can tell that the article will be about celebrities.*

Ask students to use the title, first paragraph, subtitles, and captions to make a prediction.

Conduct a Guided Reading Read the article to students as they follow along. Pause after each section to monitor students' comprehension.

- Have students pause to ask questions as they read.
- Call on volunteers to answer students' questions.

Reflect on the Article After reading the article, review ideas introduced before or during reading.

- Ask students what information they would like to add to their Real-Life Connection organizers.
- Have students look at their predictions and evaluate whether they were accurate.

Practice and Apply

Discuss the Questions Gauge students' comprehension and help them develop critical reading skills. (Answer Key, p. 126)

Connect to the Big Question Use the Making Personal Connections Organizer to have students answer the BQ.

- Have students write the topic *People's fascination with celebrity life* in the top box. Have students brainstorm personal experiences and connections to the topic and write them in the correct boxes.
- Direct students to use their organizers to help them respond to the BQ. Have students use examples in their responses.

Assess

To informally assess, have students create their own quizzes about the article.

- Divide students into groups of five. Have each student in the group write a question. Group members should not duplicate one another's questions.
- Have groups trade questions, with each student independently answering the five questions on their own paper.
- Collect and assess answers.

Reach All Learners

Build Fluency Choose a section from the article for an Echo Reading.

- Read the section one sentence at a time, emphasizing grouping words into phrases.
- Have students echo read the sentence after you, imitating your phrasing.

Use Small Groups To engage students in active learning, have them write mock news reports about a positive and a negative celebrity.

- Have groups of four collaborate in writing their news reports.
- Direct students to choose the media in which their report will appear, such as TV, newspaper, or Web site.
- Remind students that the reports should grab the audience's attention and provide answers to "5 Ws and an H" questions.
- Share reports in a class discussion.

Assist Students Having Difficulty If students struggle to grasp the overall points of the article, have them retell smaller sections.

- Ask the student to read a section and then retell it in his or her own words.
- Make notes of the student's retelling. Have the student use the notes to summarize the entire article.

WRITING JOURNAL

Extend

Write About It Students will use a T-Chart and write an advice column for teens.

- Read and discuss the Writing Prompt. (Journal, p. 128) Review the Writing Rubric.
- Encourage students to add more points to the rubric to guide their work.
- Model how to use the organizer.
- Students should use the Check It and Fix It and the Writing Checklist to revise and evaluate their work.

Model drafting by thinking aloud:

> **THINK ALOUD** *I want to be sure that I make an argument that I can actually support with strong reasons from the article. To do that, I am going to see which column—Good Reasons or Bad Reasons—has the best support for my argument. Then I will make sure all the reasons I have listed really are good or bad reasons.*

Vocabulary Workshop Students extend their thinking about Word Bank words.

- Students work in pairs or small groups on the Define It organizer. (Journal, p. 130)
- Have students add words to the Your Choice box and their personal word bank.
- Use the Show You Know exercise to assess students' understanding.

Teaching Tip Write the word part *-ology* on a poster along with its definition. Explain to students that because it means "study of," this word part is often used with sciences, school subjects, and medicine. Have students use examples from the Word Part activity and other words they brainstorm to add to the poster. Have them draw pictures next to the word parts, such as a heart for *cardio-* or a person for *anthro-*, to reinforce meaning.

The Age Factor

PROGRAM RESOURCES

ANTHOLOGY pp. 140–143

TEACHING GUIDE AND RESOURCES
- Two-Column Journal **p. 153**
- Answer Key **p. 126**

REAL WORLD WRITING JOURNAL pp. 132–135

ANTHOLOGY

Preteach

Activate Prior Knowledge Have students answer the question in the Real-Life Connection. Students will revisit answers after they read.

Build Background *Some professional sports have minimum age limits for players. For example, the NBA allows people nineteen years old and older to play professional basketball; they do not, however, have a maximum age limit. Some other types of workers, such as pilots, firefighters, and police officers, must stop working by a certain age.*

Introduce Vocabulary

- Have student pairs take turns reading the Word Bank words and definitions.
- Direct students to use each word in a new sentence about themselves. For example, *I want to **teach** my brother to play basketball.*
- *Build Academic Vocabulary* Ask groups to explain how they might use *inform* or *speak* in another subject.

Teach

Focus on the Big Question Ask the Article BQ, "What message about aging do older athletes communicate?" Students will answer this question after reading.

- *Connect to the Unit Big Question* Pair students and have them discuss how the Article and Unit BQs are similar and different.

Preread the Article Before students read, have them scan the article to predict.

- Have students read the title, subheadings, and first sentences of each section.
- Tell students to scan the article for proper nouns, such as the names of people and teams.
- Ask students to write a short prediction.

Conduct a Guided Reading Read the article to students as they follow along. Pause after each section to monitor students' comprehension.

- Give each student a copy of the Two-Column Journal to fill out as they read. Model how to use the organizer:

> **THINK ALOUD** *The first part tells that Jim Morris decided to follow his dream at the age of thirty-five. I know that is an important part of the article, so I will write that in the left column. It must have been hard to leave his family and teaching job to take a big risk. I will add my thoughts in the "My Thoughts" column.*

Reflect on the Article After reading the article, review ideas introduced before or during reading.

- Have students revisit their answers to the Real-Life Connection. Have their answers changed? Ask students why.
- Have students evaluate their predictions.

Practice and Apply

Discuss the Questions Gauge students' comprehension and help them develop critical reading skills. (Answer Key, p. 126)

Connect to the Big Question Have students review their completed Two-Column Journals and use the information to help answer the question.

- Have students write the Article BQ on their organizers. Provide a sentence frame to help students respond: *The athletes described in the article show that age ….*
- Call for volunteers to share their answers.

Assess

Play a game to informally assess student learning.

- Give each student two slips of paper. Have students write one true statement and one false statement about information from the article. Have students mark the statements *T* or *F*.
- Collect the slips of paper and divide students into teams.
- Draw a slip of paper and read the statement. Have groups confer and answer *T* or *F*.

Reach All Learners

Build Fluency Choose a quotation from the article to practice fluency.

- Have students follow along as you read aloud.
- Point out that quoted material sounds different from surrounding text.
- Have pairs practice reading the quotations. Have partners provide feedback on whether the reader sounded like a person talking.

Use Small Groups Students write an analysis to understand the issues raised in the article.

- Tell students they will write a recommendation to a professional sports team about whether they should hire an older or a younger athlete.
- Organize students into groups of four. Groups may use information from the article.
- Have groups share their recommendations with the class.

Assist Students Having Difficulty If students struggle to determine important information in the article, provide them with sticky notes.

- Find a detail in the article. Model for students evaluating whether the detail is important to the main idea or just interesting.
- Have students record details using the sticky notes as they read. At the end of the article, have them evaluate the importance of the details, removing sticky notes for facts that are interesting but not important.

WRITING JOURNAL

Extend

Write About It Students will use an Opinion and Reasons Organizer and write a debate position about older athletes.

- Read and discuss the Writing Prompt. (Journal, p. 132) Review the Writing Rubric.
- Encourage students to add more points to the rubric to guide their work.
- Model how to use the organizer.
- Students should use the Check It and Fix It and the Writing Checklist to revise and evaluate their work.

Teaching Tip Explain to students that in a debate, people present opposite views about a topic. After each person presents his or her arguments, the speakers discuss why they disagree. Find students with opposite views on the topic. Have them present their debates. As a class, discuss how each person could make his or her argument stronger.

Vocabulary Workshop Students extend their thinking about Word Bank words.

- Students work in pairs or small groups on the Define It organizer. (Journal, p. 134)
- Have students add words to the Your Choice box and their personal word bank.
- Use the Show You Know exercise to assess students' understanding.

Model making connections by thinking aloud:

> **THINK ALOUD** *As I look at the words, I wonder what connections I can make. I see the words* inform *and* teach *on the list. Both of those words are about learning, so I will make a connection between them. In the Connection box, I write, "Both are about learning and giving people knowledge about something."*

What is the best way to communicate?

Introduce the Unit Project

TV Commercial Students will create a TV commercial presenting an answer to the Big Question: *What is the best way to communicate?*

- Read through the steps of the assignment with students.
- Point out the rubric so that students will know their goals for the assignment. Add other rubric points with students to guide their work.
- Allow time for students to practice and present their work. Encourage listeners to offer their feedback and advice on the commercial.

Model Model how to make sure the main idea is clear by thinking aloud:

> **THINK ALOUD** *I am not positive that the main idea of my commercial is clear. I know that the purpose of a commercial is to "sell" something—whether a product or an idea. I am "selling" the idea of the best way to communicate, so that needs to be clearer. I can change the wording so that it tells people directly what the best way is to communicate.*

Teaching Tip TV commercials need to catch viewers' attention quickly and keep viewers interested. As a class, brainstorm ideas for making the commercials attention-grabbing. Have students think of a good commercial and the features that make it interesting, such as music, nice scenery, cool product features, or humor. Ask students then to consider what features are appropriate for their messages.

Conclude the Unit

Review Unit Objectives Return to the unit objectives and ask students to evaluate how well they mastered each one on a scale of 1 to 5, with 1 being low and 5 being high. Discuss how lower scores could be improved.

Reflect on the Learning Examine the bulletin board with students. Ask them to reflect on what they have learned. They can write or discuss with the class or in small groups. Ask questions such as:

- What was the most interesting article you read? What did you like about it?
- How did your ideas about good ways to communicate change?
- Which topic would you like to know more about?
- How did the writing assignments and the TV commercial help you form your ideas about communication?
- What would you tell a friend who asked you the Big Question: *What is the best way to communicate?*

Name _____

Word Bank Quiz

WORD LIST A			
communicate	express	media	technology
enrich	inform	paraphrase	translate
entertain	listen	speak	transmit

Ten of the unit Word Bank words are defined in parentheses in the article below. As you read the article, use Word List A, above, to figure out which word best fits each definition. Write the word on the line provided. (You will not use every word on the list.) Then go on to the next page of the quiz.

Cell Phones: For Fun or Safety?

Many teenagers think cell phones are a great way to **(1. give or receive information)**

_____ with family and friends. In the past, people used cell phones

just to **(2. use your voice to talk)** _____ to other people. Today,

people use cell phones to send text messages, take pictures, and **(3. pay attention**

to what you hear) _____ to music. New displays and features

even allow the phones to **(4. hold people's interest)** _____

users with video clips and access to **(5. communication that reaches many people)**

_____ like the Internet and radio. Some people use cell phones to

(6. show your feelings) _____ themselves with unusual ring tones

or colorful styles.

The features on cell phones **(7. make better)** _____ many

teenagers' lives by letting them stay in touch. Today's cell phones may come with

new **(8. science that solves problems)** _____, however, that

teens do not like. Some phones use GPS, global positioning systems, to **(9. send)**

_____ information about where the cell phone is. These phones can

(10. give knowledge to) _____ parents about where their kids are.

WORD LIST B			
argue	describe	produce	reveal
contribute	learn	react	source
copy	method	relate	teach

Ten more Word Bank words are defined in parentheses in the rest of the article, below. As you read the article, use Word List B, above, to figure out which word best fits each definition. Write the word on the line provided. (You will not use every word on the list.)

Parents may believe that using GPS can **(11. make)** _____

positive results. Teens, however, may not **(12. give details about)**

_____ the situation in the same way. Using GPS can be

a **(13. a place where something begins)** _____ of conflict between

parents and children. GPS can be used in cars today as well as in cell phones. GPS

in cars can tell parents how fast the car is going and where it has been. Parents do

not always **(14. show something that was hidden)** _____ that

their kids' phones or cars have GPS. When some teens **(15. get new information**

about) _____ about the GPS, they may feel like their parents

are spying on them. Teens may **(16. take action in response to something)**

_____ in a negative way. They may find a **(17. way of doing**

something) _____ to avoid being "watched," such as turning

a phone off or leaving it somewhere.

Many teens **(18. give reasons for or against an idea)** _____ that

they have a right to privacy. On the other hand, parents try to **(19. explain information**

to) _____ their children to make smart decisions and safe choices

in the world. These parents believe using GPS can **(20. do or give to reach a goal)**

_____ to the safety of their children.

 # Do others see us more clearly than we see ourselves?

Unit Overview

Students will read about attitude and working with others and examine how both can create a sense of purpose. But when the topic is harassment or self-destructive behavior, one's attitude can have a very different effect. Students consider perspective and self-awareness in this unit to decide how they'll recognize their own unique points of view.

Launch the Unit

Connect to the Big Question Read the introduction with students and examine the illustration. Ask questions such as:

- *What are some ways people see themselves? How do you see yourself?*
- *What do you think is the student's opinion of the artwork?*
- *What does the teacher's comment tell you about her opinion?*
- *Describe a similar situation you may have had with a teacher or coach.*
- *How do others help us take risks we might not normally take?*

Use the prompt on the page as the basis for journal writing or for small group or whole class discussion. Students can share their ideas with partners or in small groups.

Anchor Students' Thinking Post the Big Question on a bulletin board. Students can add to it throughout the unit. Use ideas such as the following:

- Have students illustrate goals they'd like to achieve and post their illustrations.
- Brainstorm ideas of charitable contributions students can make or good works students can do locally.
- Encourage students to do random acts of kindness for classmates. Tell students to describe the kindnesses they received on index cards and post the cards on the board.
- Set aside a problem-solving corner on the board. Allow students to anonymously post problems around the school they could help solve, and lead a class discussion about solutions.

Unit Objectives

Share these objectives with students. As you read the articles in this unit, you will:

- Consider how one's attitude influences their feelings and choices.
- Determine an answer to the Big Question: *Do others see us more clearly than we see ourselves?* Explain your answers using details from the articles and from your own experiences.
- Use vocabulary to talk and write about conflict.
- Write, discuss, and summarize your ideas about the Big Question with a group.

UNIT 5

How Attitude Helps

PROGRAM RESOURCES

ANTHOLOGY pp. 148–151

TEACHING GUIDE AND RESOURCES
- Making Personal Connections Organizer **p. 147**
- Answer Key **p. 128**

REAL WORLD WRITING JOURNAL pp. 138–141

ANTHOLOGY

Preteach

Activate Prior Knowledge Read aloud the Real-Life Connection to students. Have students record *True* or *False* for each statement. Students will revisit answers after they read.

Build Background *When you see a glass of water that is filled halfway, would you describe the glass of water as half-full or half-empty? It's thought that a person who describes the glass as half-full looks on the positive side of life, whereas a person who describes the glass as half-empty may tend toward negativity.*

Introduce Vocabulary

- Have students read each Word Bank word with a partner and discuss which words are familiar and which words are new to them.
- Read the example for each word. Have volunteers suggest a synonym for each.
- *Build Academic Vocabulary* Work with students to identify academic vocabulary words. Have students suggest a sentence for each word.

Teach

Focus on the Big Question Ask the Article BQ, "Do negative thoughts keep you down?" Students will answer this question after reading.

- *Connect to the Unit Big Question* Write the Unit and Article BQs on the board. Have students suggest similarities and differences between the two questions.

Preread the Article Before students read, model how to preview and predict:

THINK ALOUD *The title is "How Attitude Helps." The subtitles are in bold at the top of each section. "Self-Help," "Empowering," "True Focus," and*

"Making Your Own Choices" are the subtitles. I predict the article might be about how we can help improve our attitudes.

Ask students to write their own predictions.

Conduct a Guided Reading Read the article to the students as they follow along. Pause after each section to monitor students' comprehension.

- Have students ask a question after reading each section.
- Ask students to identify the main idea of each section and the article.

Reflect on the Article After reading the article, review ideas introduced before or during reading.

- Revisit the True/False statements from the Real-Life Connection. Have answers changed? Ask students why.
- Ask students to evaluate their predictions.

Practice and Apply

Discuss the Questions Gauge students' comprehension and help them develop critical reading skills. (Answer Key, p. 128)

Connect to the Big Question Have students use the Making Personal Connections Organizer to answer the BQ.

- Have students write the Article BQ on their organizers. Tell students to write what is being explained in the article in the top box.
- Have students work independently to describe the connections to their personal experience and to other media. Then discuss the BQ, allowing students to refer to their organizers.

Assess

Have students participate in a role play for you to informally assess. Organize students into small groups and have them write a brief scene that shows a situation in which maintaining a positive attitude would be helpful. Tell students their role plays might also show how a negative attitude would result in a different outcome. Ask groups to perform their role plays for the class.

Reach All Learners

Build Fluency Choose a section from the article for an Echo Reading.

- Read the section aloud to students, modeling reading with accuracy.
- Have the class read the same section aloud as a group, focusing on accuracy.
- Tell students to repeat the process with partners. The first partner reads a section aloud, focusing on accuracy, and the second partner echo reads.

Use Small Groups Engage students in a discussion to extend the theme of the article.

- Point out that the article references the growth of the self-help industry. Have students discuss what they think of when they hear the term *self-help*.
- Tell students to work in groups and brainstorm a list of issues and questions that kids and teenagers need help with. Ask students to suggest places where they might find answers.
- Have each group share its ideas with the class. Discuss the issues most groups had in common, and why they are important to kids today.

Assist Students Having Difficulty If students struggle to speak in front of the class, provide them with support.

- Encourage students to take a small speaking part in the role-play activity.
- Have students practice reading aloud with partners by Echo Reading.

WRITING JOURNAL

Extend

Write About It Students will use a notepad graphic organizer to plan and write a diary entry.

- Read and discuss the Writing Prompt. (Journal, p. 138) Review the Writing Rubric. Encourage students to add more points to the rubric to guide their work.
- Model how to use the organizer.
- Students should use the Check It and Fix It Section and the Writing Checklist to revise and evaluate their work.

Model organizing by thinking aloud:

> **THINK ALOUD** *I want to be sure that I explain the reasons behind my attitude. I think of examples from my daily life and write them on the notepad. I also include ideas from the article that support my reasons in my diary entry.*

Vocabulary Workshop Students extend their thinking about Word Bank words.

- Students work in pairs or small groups on the Define It organizer. (Journal, p. 140)
- Have students add words to the Your Choice box and their personal word bank.
- Use the Show You Know exercise to assess students' understanding.

Teaching Tip After finishing the academic vocabulary activity independently, have students work in small groups to share their examples of the various uses for academic vocabulary words. Ask groups to report the total number of uses they discovered with the whole group. List the different uses on the board as groups share their responses.

Happiness: A Two-Way Street?

PROGRAM RESOURCES

ANTHOLOGY pp. 152–155

TEACHING GUIDE AND RESOURCES
- T-Chart p. 151
- Main Idea Map p. 146
- Answer Key p. 128

REAL WORLD WRITING JOURNAL pp. 142–145

ANTHOLOGY

Preteach

Activate Prior Knowledge Draw the word web from the Real-Life Connection on chart paper and complete it with students. Students will revisit answers after they read.

Build Background *Abraham Lincoln once said, "People are about as happy as they make up their minds to be." He meant that it is possible to choose happiness. In this article, we will read about people who choose happiness by helping others.*

Introduce Vocabulary

- Have students read the words and definitions in the Word Bank. Ask volunteers to identify a synonym for each word.
- Display or distribute the T-Chart. Tell students to choose two words from the Word Bank and list synonyms for each word.
- *Build Academic Vocabulary* Point out the academic vocabulary words in the Word Bank and ask students to suggest other places they might read these words. Have volunteers suggest how they could use these words in conversation.

Teach

Focus on the Big Question Ask the Article BQ, "What does it take to be happy?" Students will answer this question after reading.

- *Connect to the Unit Big Question* Have students read the Unit and Article BQs with a partner. Have them discuss connections between the two questions.

Preread the Article Before students read, model how to preview and predict:

THINK ALOUD *On the first page of the article, I see builders. The caption says they are working for Habitat for Humanity. On the second page, I see one person helping another. I think this article will include information about how helping others gives people a feeling of happiness.*

Ask students to make other predictions about the article based on photos and captions.

Conduct a Guided Reading Read the article to students as they follow along. Pause after each section to monitor students' comprehension.

- Ask "5 Ws and an H" questions.
- Have students make connections to real-world examples as they read.

Reflect on the Article After reading the article, review ideas introduced before or during reading.

- Revisit the word web chart. Have students add words they thought of while reading.
- Have volunteers explain how they could change or improve their predictions.

Practice and Apply

Discuss the Questions Gauge students' comprehension and help them develop critical reading skills. (Answer Key, p. 128)

Connect to the Big Question Have students use the Main Idea Map to answer the BQ.

- Have students write the main idea and supporting details on their maps. Encourage students to refer back to the article for supporting events and details.
- Remind students of the Article BQ. Ask a volunteer to read the BQ aloud. Then have students suggest answers, using the ideas from their organizers for support.

Assess

Have students create a learning log for you to informally assess. Students should answer these questions:

- What did you learn about happiness from the article?
- What did you find most interesting?
- What questions do you still have? In what sources could you find answers?

Reach All Learners

Build Fluency Choose a section from the article for a Paired Reading.

- Pair students and have them read silently.
- Tell one student to read aloud as the partner follows and makes notes.
- Have listeners provide suggestions and feedback based on their notes. Students then reverse roles.

Use Small Groups Engage students in a think/pair/share activity.

- Organize students in small groups and assign each group one of the Use Clues questions.
- Have students think about their answer to the question. Then have students pair with a group member to discuss ideas. Finally, have each student share his or her ideas with the group.
- Direct one student in each group to act as reporter. Ask the reporter to share the group's answer with the whole class.

Assist Students Having Difficulty If students struggle to make predictions, explain how considering the topic can help.

- Point out that making a prediction is like making a good guess about what will happen in the article based on clues in the text.
- Tell students to think about what they already know about a topic when they make a prediction.

WRITING JOURNAL

Extend

Write About It Students will use a concept web to plan and write a treatment for a reality show.

- Read and discuss the Writing Prompt. (Journal, p. 142) Review the Writing Rubric. Encourage students to add more points to the rubric to guide their work.
- Model how to use the organizer.
- Students should use the Check It and Fix It Section and the Writing Checklist to revise and evaluate their work.

Model drafting by thinking aloud:

THINK ALOUD *I want to be sure that I include all the ideas on my concept web in my treatment. I will reread my ideas as I write, making a check mark next to each as I use the idea. That way I can be sure that my treatment includes all the activities from my web.*

Vocabulary Workshop Students extend their thinking about Word Bank words.

- Students work in pairs or small groups on the Define It organizer. (Journal, p. 144)
- Have students add words to the Your Choice box and their personal word bank.
- Use the Show You Know exercise to assess students' understanding.

Teaching Tip Post chart paper on a wall or bulletin board. Have students draw their comic strips from the Show You Know activity on the chart paper. As students view the comics, have them look for effective use of the vocabulary words.

Called Out

PROGRAM RESOURCES

ANTHOLOGY pp. 156–159

TEACHING GUIDE AND RESOURCES
- Guess It and Check It Chart **p. 143**
- Problem and Solution Map **p. 149**
- Answer Key **p. 128**

REAL WORLD WRITING JOURNAL pp. 146–149

ANTHOLOGY

Preteach

Activate Prior Knowledge Have students copy and complete the chart in the Real-Life Connection. Students will revisit answers after they read.

Build Background *An intervention is a serious discussion led by a professional like a doctor or therapist. If you suspect someone is engaging in self-destructive behavior, confronting them on your own is not always the best idea. Sometimes asking a trusted adult for help is the best thing to do.*

Introduce Vocabulary

- Display or distribute the Guess It and Check It Chart. Have students list the Word Bank words in the first column.
- Have students work with a partner to find each word in context. Tell students to write the clues to each word's meaning and then complete the chart with word meanings.
- *Build Academic Vocabulary* Write a word web for one academic vocabulary term on the board and have students make connections to other words they know.

Teach

Focus on the Big Question Ask the Article BQ, "Why might an intervention be the best way to help someone?" Students will answer this question after reading.

- *Connect to the Unit Big Question* Write the Unit and Article BQs on the board. Have students discuss similarities between the two.

Preread the Article Before students read, model how to preview and predict:

> **THINK ALOUD** *I am going to skim the article to make a prediction about what it is about. I can read topic sentences when I preview an article for information. Topic sentences usually contain the main idea for each paragraph.*

Ask students to write a prediction.

Conduct a Guided Reading Read the article to the students as they follow along. Pause after each section to monitor students' comprehension.

- Ask students to summarize each section.
- Have students make inferences about why kids engage in self-destructive behaviors.

Reflect on the Article After reading the article, review ideas introduced before or during reading.

- Have students reread the chart from the Real-Life Connection. Ask students what they could add to their charts.
- Have students evaluate their predictions.

Practice and Apply

Discuss the Questions Gauge students' comprehension and help them develop critical reading skills. (Answer Key, p. 128)

Connect to the Big Question Use the Problem and Solution Map to have students answer the BQ.

- Have students write the Article BQ on their organizers. Students can complete the organizers with partners.
- Ask volunteers to identify the problem the article focused on. Have them discuss the possible solutions, responses, and end results. Then have students answer the BQ.

Assess

Have students write interview questions for you to informally assess. Tell students to imagine they will interview a professional who leads interventions. Have students write five questions they would like to ask this person. Tell students their questions should reflect what they learned from the article. If time allows, students can trade questions and see which questions are answered in the article.

Reach All Learners

Build Fluency Choose a section from the article for a Choral Reading.

- Read the section to students, modeling reading with expression.
- Have the class read the same section aloud as a group, focusing on reading with expression.
- Repeat the process with another section of the article.

Use Small Groups Engage students with a Role Play activity.

- Have groups discuss issues that concern them. Tell them to imagine a friend has gotten himself into a tough situation.
- Tell students to discuss appropriate ways of dealing with this situation, such as approaching the friend to share their concerns.
- Have groups write a dialogue in which they approach a friend. Tell them to include dialogue for the friend, showing his or her reaction. Ask groups to present their scenes to the whole class.

Assist Students Having Difficulty If students struggle to answer the BQ, provide them with support.

- Have students discuss their understanding of the BQ with a partner.
- Tell students to reread the article and list the benefits of intervention as they read.

WRITING JOURNAL

Extend

Write About It Students will use a T-Chart to plan and write guidelines for getting help.

- Read and discuss the Writing Prompt. (Journal, p. 146) Review the Writing Rubric. Encourage students to add more points to the rubric to guide their work.
- Model how to use the organizer.
- Students should use the Check It and Fix It Section and the Writing Checklist to revise and evaluate their work.

Model revising by thinking aloud:

> **THINK ALOUD** *I want to be sure my guidelines are clear. First I will reread them aloud to check them over. If I stumble over any words, I may need to go back and fix my sentences. Then I will ask a partner to read my guidelines. I will use suggestions from my partner to rewrite, revise, and improve my writing.*

Vocabulary Workshop Students extend their thinking about Word Bank words.

- Students work in pairs or small groups on the Define It organizer. (Journal, p. 148)
- Have students add words to the Your Choice box and their personal word bank.
- Use the Show You Know exercise to assess students' understanding.

Teaching Tip Ask volunteers to read aloud the completed Word Endings paragraph with expression. Then have volunteers suggest sentences with the words they did not use that have the same meaning, such as "Our opinions differ" and "Our opinions are different" for the first sentence.

Pushing Buttons

PROGRAM RESOURCES

ANTHOLOGY pp. 160–163

TEACHING GUIDE AND RESOURCES
- Cause and Effect Map **p. 140**
- Venn Diagram **p. 154**
- Answer Key **p. 129**

REAL WORLD WRITING JOURNAL pp. 150–153

ANTHOLOGY

Preteach

Activate Prior Knowledge Read aloud the Real-Life Connection to students. Have students record *True* or *False* for each statement. Students will revisit answers after they read.

Build Background *The Internet has made it quick and easy to send e-mail, chat, or IM a friend. Unfortunately, the Internet has also provided bullies with a new way to harass others. In this article, we will read about cyberbullying and how you can protect yourself.*

Introduce Vocabulary

- Have students scan the article to find sentences with boldface vocabulary words. Ask volunteers to read these sentences aloud.
- Tell students to work in pairs to write a definition for each word. Then have students compare their definitions with those on p. 160.
- *Build Academic Vocabulary* Write the academic vocabulary words on index cards. Have volunteers pick a card and use the word in a sentence.

Teach

Focus on the Big Question Ask the Article BQ, "What is the best way to handle hurtful gossip?" Students will answer this question after reading.

- *Connect to the Unit Big Question* Have students read the Unit and Article BQs. Discuss how gossip might affect the way a person sees himself or herself.

Preread the Article Before students read, model how to preview and predict:

> **THINK ALOUD** *The introduction to the article appears above the title. The title of this article is "Pushing Buttons." The introduction and the title make me think this article is about people gossiping over the Internet.*

Ask students to write a prediction.

Conduct a Guided Reading Read the article to the students as they follow along. Pause after each section to monitor students' comprehension.

- Have students identify facts about cyberbullying as they read.
- Ask students to compare and contrast online bullying with physical bullying.

Reflect on the Article After reading the article, review ideas introduced before or during reading.

- Revisit the True/False statements from the Real-Life Connection. Ask students if their opinions have changed.
- Tell students to reread their predictions and discuss ideas they would change.

Practice and Apply

Discuss the Questions Gauge students' comprehension and help them develop critical reading skills. (Answer Key, p. 129)

Connect to the Big Question Have students use the Cause and Effect Map to answer the BQ.

- Have students write the Article BQ on their organizers. Identify the cause, *cyberbullying*. Tell students to write the word and its definition in the center circle.
- Have students work with a partner to identify three effects of cyberbullying. Then discuss the answer to the BQ.

Assess

Have students create a pop-up ad for you to informally assess. Students should design a pop-up ad that would appear on the computer screen whenever a cyberbully writes an insulting message. Tell students their pop-up ad should be a persuasive message that would inform the cyberbully about what he or she was doing and convince the cyberbully to change his or her behavior.

Reach All Learners

Build Fluency Choose a section from the article for an Echo Reading.

- Read the section aloud to students, modeling reading with expression.
- Have the class read the same section aloud as a group, focusing on reading with expression.
- Tell students to repeat the process with a partner. The first partner reads a section aloud with expression and the second partner echo reads.

Use Small Groups Engage students with a Write-Around activity.

- In groups of four, have each student begin with a piece of paper with the Article BQ written across the top.
- Have students write a response for one minute and then pass their papers to the right. The one-minute writing begins again, and students add to the paper in front of them responding to the idea that is already there.
- Continue until all students have written on each paper. Discuss with the class.

Assist Students Having Difficulty If students struggle to compare and contrast cyberbullying and physical bullying, provide them with support.

- Distribute a Venn Diagram for organizing ideas.
- Have students work with a partner to write the similarities and differences between the two kinds of bullying.

WRITING JOURNAL

Extend

Write About It Students will use a notepad graphic organizer to plan and write a letter.

- Read and discuss the Writing Prompt. (Journal, p. 150) Review the Writing Rubric. Encourage students to add more points to the rubric to guide their work.
- Model how to use the organizer.
- Students should use the Check It and Fix It Section and the Writing Checklist to revise and evaluate their work.

Model organizing ideas by thinking aloud:

> **THINK ALOUD** *I will start by writing my opinion about cyberbullying on the organizer. I think cyberbullies should be stopped. Next I will list reasons from the article and my notes that support my opinion. I will review these reasons when it is time to write my letter.*

Vocabulary Workshop Students extend their thinking about Word Bank words.

- Students work in pairs or small groups on the Define It organizer. (Journal, p. 152)
- Have students add words to the Your Choice box and their personal word bank.
- Use the Show You Know exercise to assess students' understanding.

Teaching Tip Review with students the words they came up with for the All in the Family activity. Have volunteers write the various forms of *identify* on the board. Then ask students to write an original sentence for each new word. Have students share their sentences with the class.

Do others see us more clearly than we see ourselves?

Introduce the Unit Project

Write-Around Students will participate in a write-around, discussing and summarizing an answer to the Big Question: *Do others see us more clearly than we see ourselves?*

- Read through the steps of the assignment with students.
- Point out the rubric so that students will know their goals for the assignment. Add other rubric points with students to guide their work.
- Allow time for students to practice and present their work. Encourage listeners to offer their feedback and advice on the presentation.

Model Model how to plan a complete response by thinking aloud.

> **THINK ALOUD** *As I check my work, I will review the viewpoints of all group members. The different group members had various points of view. I will make sure that everyone's point of view is represented in our summary. If anyone disagreed, I can include the ideas we disagreed about in the summary and explain them in the presentation.*

Teaching Tip Students will have to draw conclusions in order to answer the Big Question. Point out that while the question is not answered directly in the articles, all the article topics address the idea of how one sees oneself. Encourage students to draw logical conclusions as they discuss their answers to the Big Question.

Conclude the Unit

Review Unit Objectives Return to the unit objectives and ask students to evaluate how well they mastered each one on a scale of 1 to 5, with 1 being low and 5 being high. Discuss how lower scores could be improved.

Reflect on the Learning Examine the bulletin board with students. Ask them to reflect on what they have learned. They can write or discuss with the class or in small groups. Ask questions such as:

- What was the most interesting article you read? What did you like about it?

- How did your ideas about perspective change as you read through the articles?
- Which topic would you like to know more about? What do you still wonder about it?
- How did the writing assignments and the interview help you form your ideas about who sees the real you?
- What connections did you make between the ideas in the articles and your own life?

Name _____

Word Bank Quiz

WORD LIST A			
appearance	characteristics	identify	perception
appreciate	consider	ignore	perspectives
assumption	focus	image	reveal

Ten of the unit Word Bank words are defined in parentheses in the article below. As you read the article, use Word List A, above, to figure out which word best fits each definition. Write the word on the line provided. (You will not use every word on the list.) Then go on to the next page of the quiz.

Behind the Mask

How do you get to know a person? How do you decide who sees the real you?

(1. Think carefully about) _____ the many ways people make

judgments about one another. What we value in others can **(2. show something that**

was hidden) _____ what we think is important in life.

Loyalty, honesty, and a good sense of humor are all **(3. traits)**

_____ that many people **(4. value)** _____

in a friend. However, do not make the **(5. something you suppose is true)**

_____ that everyone values the same things. Different people can

have different **(6. points of view)** _____.

For some people, it is all about **(7. a mental picture)** _____.

Sometimes we may judge a person based on their **(8. outward looks)**

_____. This is just another way we form our **(9. what you see or**

understand) _____ of a person. It is important not to **(10. pay no**

attention) _____ the other qualities that make a person unique.

When we concentrate on looks alone, we may miss the chance to really get to know

someone.

UNIT 5 Word Bank Quiz

WORD LIST B			
appearance	consider	focus	reflect
bias	define	perspectives	reveal
complete	identify	reaction	setting

Ten more Word Bank words are defined in parentheses in the story below. As you read the story, use Word List B, above, to figure out which word best fits each definition. Write the word on the line provided. (You will not use every word on the list.)

Seeing below the surface is the only way to get a **(11. finished)**

_____ picture of a person. Deciding on who will be a friend based

only on a person's physical **(12. outward looks)** _____ alone is

unfair. Every individual must let go of any **(13. like or dislike that prevents them from**

being fair) _____ they hold in order to get to know people who

appear different at first.

It takes time to really get to know someone. When you first meet someone,

similar interests **(14. demonstrate)** _____ a common bond. The

(15. where the action takes place) _____ where you met a person

may influence your connection to a new friend. Maybe you had the same **(16. response)**

_____ to a shared experience.

Whatever the circumstances, you are most likely to connect with people who **(17. give**

an exact meaning) _____ friendship in similar terms. You may have

differences, but you can **(18. recognize)** _____ the things you have

in common. People with similar **(19. points of view)** _____ often

become friends. When you **(20. concentrate)** _____ only on the

differences you have with a person, it will not lead to friendship.

Community or individual—which is more important?

Unit Overview

The articles in this unit explore the topic of communities and individuals. As students read about balancing the needs of individuals and communities, they will analyze how individuals act can affect an entire community and, likewise, how a community influences the lives of the individuals living within it.

Launch the Unit

Connect to the Big Question Read the introduction with students and examine the illustration. Ask questions such as:

- *What are some examples of different kinds of communities?*
- *Do you think the teen in the photograph thinks the individual or the community is more important?*
- *How does the teen in the photograph express her individuality?*
- *Do you think Americans value individuals or communities more? Why?*

Use the prompt on the page as the basis for journal writing or for small group or whole class discussion. Students can share their ideas with partners or in small groups.

Anchor Students' Thinking Start a unit chart with the Big Question at the top. Use these ideas for column headings. Have students add to it throughout the unit.

- *Community or Individual?* Ask students whether each article is about the needs of individuals, communities, or both. Students post ideas.
- *Words* Have students add vocabulary words that can be used to talk about communities and individuals.
- *Personal Connection* Have students identify connections to the articles.
- *In the World* Encourage students to add examples of how individuals and communities interact, such as newspaper or magazine articles.

Unit Objectives

Share these objectives with students. As you read the articles in this unit, you will:

- Identify issues affecting communities and the individuals within them.
- Determine an answer to the Big Question: *Community or individual—which is more important?* Explain your answers using details from the articles and from your own experiences.
- Use vocabulary words to talk and write about communities and individuals.
- Work with a partner to answer the Big Question and conduct an interview.

The Great Dress Debate

PROGRAM RESOURCES

ANTHOLOGY pp. 168–171

TEACHING GUIDE AND RESOURCES
- Cause and Effect Map p. 140
- Answer Key p. 130

REAL WORLD WRITING JOURNAL pp. 156–159

ANTHOLOGY

Preteach

Activate Prior Knowledge Have students complete the chart from Real-Life Connection. Students will revisit answers after they read.

Build Background *During the 2005–2006 school year, about 14 percent of public school principals reported that their schools required uniforms. When uniforms are required, it is usually at the elementary, middle, and junior high school levels.*

Introduce Vocabulary

- Write the Word Bank words on the board. Have students scan the article for sentences where the boldface words appear.
- Tell students to look for clues in the sentences about what each word means.
- *Build Academic Vocabulary* All the Word Bank words are academic vocabulary. Ask students to explain how they might use the words in a social studies class.

Teach

Focus on the Big Question Ask the Article BQ, "Is individuality more important than following the rules?" Students will answer this question after reading.

- *Connect to the Unit Big Question* Write the Unit and Article BQs on the board. Point out the lesson vocabulary word *individual* and its variation. Ask pairs to discuss why communities have rules.

Preread the Article Before students read, have them preview the article.

- Tell students that reading the first and last paragraphs of an article can often help them understand what the article is about.
- Ask students to compare these paragraphs and write a short prediction about the article.

Conduct a Guided Reading Read the article to students as they follow along. Pause after each section to monitor students' comprehension.

- Call on a volunteer to summarize each section.
- Ask students how the table on p. 170 helps them understand school dress codes. Model interpreting the table:

> **THINK ALOUD** *From the title, I see the table is about school dress rules. I can see that the rules are arranged from the highest to the lowest percentage. Most students agreed that gang clothes should not be allowed, but few students wanted uniforms. I am going to use this information to help me understand the rest of the article.*

Reflect on the Article After reading the article, review ideas introduced before or during reading.

- Have students revisit their charts from the Real-Life Connection. Have their views changed? Ask students why.
- Ask students whether they made changes to their predictions. Have them explain why.

Practice and Apply

Discuss the Questions Gauge students' comprehension and help them develop critical reading skills. (Answer Key, p. 130)

Connect to the Big Question Have students use the Cause and Effect Map to answer the BQ.

- Have students write the Article BQ on their organizers. Provide suggestions for causes that are discussed in the article, such as *gang violence increased* or *schools required uniforms*.
- Have students look for effects. Students use their organizers to answer the BQ.

Assess

Assess students' understanding by having them write debate positions in favor of dress codes and uniforms and opposed to dress codes and uniforms. Check debates to look for ideas from the article.

Reach All Learners

Build Fluency Choose a section of the article with multiple punctuation marks (commas, periods, question marks, quotation marks) and instruct pairs to practice fluency by reading with phrasing.

- Model reading a section of the article while students listen. Ask students to make a note of the punctuation they heard.
- Pair students and have one student read while the other listens. Have the student who listens write down the punctuation he or she heard and provide feedback to the reader.

Use Small Groups Have students work in small groups to create their own school dress code policies for a school handbook.

- In groups of four, have students review the article for ideas.
- Tell students to write an introductory paragraph explaining the reason for having a dress code.
- Have students list what they want to include in their dress codes.
- Have each group share its dress codes in a class discussion and explain their thinking.

Assist Students Having Difficulty If students struggle with summarizing the two main viewpoints in the article, review what a summary is.

- Explain that a summary includes the main idea and most important ideas of an article.
- Use an overhead transparency to write the main viewpoints discussed in the article.
- Ask students to help you fill in the important details for each viewpoint.
- Review the summaries of each viewpoint on the transparency. Ask students if they want to add or remove any of the details.

WRITING JOURNAL

Extend

Write About It Students will use a T-Chart to write a meeting agenda.

- Read and discuss the Writing Prompt. (Journal, p. 156) Review the Writing Rubric. Encourage students to add more points to the rubric to guide their work.
- Model how to use the organizer.
- Students should use the Check It and Fix It Section and the Writing Checklist to revise and evaluate their work.

Model drafting by thinking aloud:

> **THINK ALOUD** *Since a meeting agenda is the schedule for how topics will be discussed, I want to be sure the most important idea is discussed first. Is school safety or individual freedom more important? I will put the most important issue first so that there will be enough time to discuss it.*

Vocabulary Workshop Students extend their thinking about the Word Bank words.

- Students work in pairs or small groups on the Define It organizer. (Journal, p. 158)
- Have students add words to the Your Choice box and their personal word bank.
- Use the Show You Know exercise to assess students' understanding.

Teaching Tip Have the class name the parts of speech for the words in All in the Family. Write the words *noun*, *adjective*, and *verb* on the board. Remind students that a noun is a person, place, or thing; a verb is an action word; and an adjective is a describing word.

Commanding the Weather

PROGRAM RESOURCES

ANTHOLOGY pp. 172–175

TEACHING GUIDE AND RESOURCES
- Main Idea Map **p. 146**
- Answer Key **p. 130**
REAL WORLD WRITING JOURNAL pp. 160–163

ANTHOLOGY

Preteach

Activate Prior Knowledge Take a poll of *True* and *False* for each question in the Real-Life Connection. Students will revisit after reading.

Build Background *Many scientists believe that global warming is contributing to increased droughts, flooding, severe weather, and warmer temperatures worldwide. Reducing pollution from vehicles and power plants are the two main ways scientists believe global warming can be reduced.*

Introduce Vocabulary

- Read aloud the Word Bank words, definitions, and example sentences.
- Ask students to think of synonyms for each word. Have students practice substituting the synonyms for the boldface words.
- *Build Academic Vocabulary* Work with students to locate academic vocabulary in the text. Discuss with students how these words relate to community.

Teach

Focus on the Big Question Ask the Article BQ, "Should we try to control the weather or let nature take its course?" Students will answer this question after reading.

- *Connect to the Unit Big Question* Write the Unit and Article BQs on the board. As a class, brainstorm ideas about how the weather affects individuals and communities.

Preread the Article Before students read, model how to preview and make predictions:

> **THINK ALOUD** *I will start with the title since it usually contains the main topic: "Commanding the Weather." The picture just below shows lightning, and the caption asks whether I would control the weather. I think the article will be about ways to control weather.*

Model how to preview other text features. Ask students to write a prediction.

Conduct a Guided Reading Read the article to students as they follow along. Pause after each section to monitor students' comprehension.

- Provide each student with a Main Idea Map. As you read, have students add main ideas and supporting details to their organizers.
- Call on volunteers to share their main ideas and supporting details.

Reflect on the Article After reading the article, review ideas introduced before or during reading.

- Retake the poll from the Real-Life Connection. Have answers changed? Ask students why.
- Ask students how what they learned was different from what they predicted. Have them suggest reasons for the discrepancy.

Practice and Apply

Discuss the Questions Gauge students' comprehension and help them develop critical reading skills. (Answer Key, p. 130)

Connect to the Big Question Refocus students' attention on the Article BQ.

- Write the Article BQ and draw a large T-Chart with the headings "Control the Weather" and "Let Nature Take Its Course."
- Survey students on their opinions. Record the reasons for opinions.
- Have students complete these sentence frames: *We should try to control the weather because* _____ *and We should let nature take its course because* _____.

Assess

Have students write their own assessments.

- Each student should write three multiple-choice and three short-answer test questions on a blank sheet of paper.
- Have students create answer keys for their tests on a separate piece of paper. Pair students and have them exchange and take each other's tests. They can discuss results.
- Have each student write two to three sentences describing what they learned and what they want to learn about controlling the weather.

Reach All Learners

Build Fluency Choose a section from the article to model the importance of reading in phrases to convey meaning.

- Choose a sentence with punctuation and prepositional phrases.
- Read the sentence by breaking up phrases and not following punctuation. Then read the sentence correctly. Ask students which version was easier to understand and why.
- Read another sentence aloud, using correct phrasing to convey meaning. Have students follow along as you read.
- Then have students chorally repeat the sentence, following your emphasis.

Use Small Groups Engage students with a group discussion to answer the last Use Clues question.

- Put students in groups of four. Read the question aloud to the class.
- Have students independently respond to the question. Then have students read their written responses to the rest of their group.
- Direct groups to discuss how their answers were similar or different.

Assist Students Having Difficulty If students struggle to find main ideas and important details in the article, provide them with two colors of sticky notes.

- Have students mark main ideas with one color, and important details with the other color.
- Explain that some details in an article might be interesting, but not important.
- Review the main ideas and important details students found.

WRITING JOURNAL

Extend

Write About It Students will use an Opinion and Reasons Organizer and write a letter to the editor.

- Read and discuss the Writing Prompt. (Journal, p. 160) Review the Writing Rubric. Encourage students to add more points to the rubric to guide their work.
- Model how to use the organizer.
- Students should use the Check It and Fix It Section and the Writing Checklist to revise and evaluate their work.

Teaching Tip Provide students with a list of signal words and phrases that can be used to state an opinion and support it with reasons, such as *I believe, I think, we should, because,* and *my reason for thinking this is.*

Vocabulary Workshop Students extend their thinking about the Word Bank words.

- Students work in pairs or small groups on the Define It organizer. (Journal, p. 162)
- Have students add words to the Your Choice box and to their personal word banks.
- Use the Show You Know exercise to assess students' understanding.

Model completing the Double-Duty Words exercise:

> **THINK ALOUD** *I know that the word spread has different meanings, like something you cover your bed with, something you might put on a sandwich, and something you do when you put something on top of something else. In this sentence, spread is something you do. Since it is an action word in this sentence, it must be a verb. I will write V on the line.*

UNIT 6

Restoring Cities from the Ground Up

PROGRAM RESOURCES

ANTHOLOGY pp. 176–179

TEACHING GUIDE AND RESOURCES
- Word Pyramid **p. 157**
- Making Personal Connections Organizer **p. 147**
- Answer Key **p. 130**

REAL WORLD WRITING JOURNAL pp. 164–167

ANTHOLOGY

Preteach

Activate Prior Knowledge Have students complete the chart in the Real-Life Connection. Model completing the chart with this think aloud:

> **THINK ALOUD** *I know that titles and headings often contain main ideas or hints about what the main ideas might be. I can tell from the title that this article is about cities. It also must have something to do with the ground, or what is on or in the ground, like plants or trees, so I will write that down.*

Students will revisit answers after they read.

Build Background *Today, many cities and neighborhoods are converting vacant lots into neighborhood gardens. Some gardens charge a small rent while others are free and produce food that they give to food banks and homeless shelters or sell.*

Introduce Vocabulary

- Read aloud the Word Bank words, definitions, and example sentences.
- Distribute the Word Pyramid. Have students work in pairs to complete the organizer for each word.
- *Build Academic Vocabulary* Review the meaning of *unify* with students. Ask them to name the classes or school situations in which they might use the word.

Teach

Focus on the Big Question Ask the Article BQ, "Can an urban garden really help turn a community around?" Students will answer this question after reading.

- *Connect to the Unit Big Question* Write the Unit and Article BQs on the board. Circle the word *community* in both questions. Discuss how the article might be about individuals.

Preread the Article Remind students of the predictions they made about the article.

- Have students look at the photographs and read the captions.
- Ask students to revise their predictions.
- Have students write two specific topics they think the article will address.

Conduct a Guided Reading Read the article to students as they follow along. Pause after each section to monitor students' comprehension.

- As you complete each section, call on a volunteer to read the subhead and explain how it is related to that section.
- Have another summarize the section.

Reflect on the Article After reading the article, review ideas introduced before or during reading.

- Have students refer to their prediction charts from the Real-Life Connection. Ask students if their predictions matched the article.
- Have students review the two topics they predicted the article would address.

Practice and Apply

Discuss the Questions Gauge students' comprehension and help them develop critical reading skills. (Answer Key, p. 130)

Connect to the Big Question Use the Making Personal Connections Organizer to answer the BQ.

- Have students write the Article BQ on their organizers.
- Ask students to make personal connections to what is described in the article.
- Call on volunteers to answer the BQ.

Assess

Have students create a Learning Log for you to informally assess. Students should answer these questions:

- What did you do in class today? What did you learn about restoring urban environments?
- What did you find interesting?
- Do you think an urban garden would work in your community? Why or why not?

Reach All Learners

Build Fluency Choose sections from the article for Radio Reads to practice fluency.

- Model reading a section as if you are delivering a radio or TV news report.
- Assign each student a section and have students practice reading silently. Explain that they should read as if they are delivering a radio or TV news story.
- Assist students with the pronunciation of people's names if necessary.
- Have volunteers read their section to the class.

Use Small Groups Engage students with a Write-Around activity to answer the second Use Clues question.

- In groups of four, have each student begin with a piece of paper with the question written across the top.
- Have students write a response for one minute and then pass their papers to the right. The one-minute writing begins again, and students add to the paper in front of them.
- Continue until all four students have written on each paper. Share writing in a class discussion.

Assist Students Having Difficulty If students struggle to respond to the Article BQ, help them make personal connections.

- Ask students if they have seen a neighborhood that is run-down or dangerous.
- Have students create a list of the groups mentioned in the article. Ask if any of these projects could help improve a run-down neighborhood. Have students translate their answer into a response to the Article BQ.

WRITING JOURNAL

Extend

Write About It Students will use a proposal organizer and write a proposal for the city council.

- Read and discuss the Writing Prompt. (Journal, p. 164) Review the Writing Rubric. Encourage students to add more points to the rubric to guide their work.
- Model how to use the organizer.
- Students should use the Check It and Fix It Section and the Writing Checklist to revise and evaluate their work.

Model organizing ideas:

> **THINK ALOUD** *Since I am writing a proposal, I want to make sure I have a clear idea of what I want to suggest. I will be making the proposal to the city council, so it will need to be carefully thought out. I am going to review the article for ideas about how other people used vacant lots. Then I will write a proposal that states clearly what I want the city council to do.*

Vocabulary Workshop Students extend their thinking about the Word Bank words.

- Students work in pairs or small groups on the Define It organizer. (Journal, p. 166)
- Have students add words to the Your Choice box and to their personal word banks.
- Use the Show You Know exercise to assess students' understanding.

Teaching Tip Have the class brainstorm adjectives that end in *-ous*. Use a piece of chart paper or poster board to list *-ous* words throughout the year. Begin by writing the words used in the Word Endings activity.

UNIT 6

What It Takes to Lead

PROGRAM RESOURCES

ANTHOLOGY pp. 180–183

TEACHING GUIDE AND RESOURCES
- Guess It and Check It Chart **p. 143**
- Three-Column Chart **p. 152**
- Venn Diagram **p. 154**
- Answer Key **p. 131**

REAL WORLD WRITING JOURNAL pp. 168–171

ANTHOLOGY

Preteach

Activate Prior Knowledge Have students copy and complete the chart in the Real-Life Connection. Students will revisit answers after they read.

Build Background *Some people believe that great leaders are born, not made. Others think the traits of a great leader can be learned. In fact, there are hundreds of "leadership training" programs designed to show people (often businesspeople) how to inspire and motivate others.*

Introduce Vocabulary

- Review the Word Bank words and definitions with students.
- Have student pairs use the Guess It and Check It Chart to practice finding context clues.
- Have students write the Word Bank words in the first column. Have them complete the chart.
- *Build Academic Vocabulary* All of the Word Bank words are academic vocabulary. Ask students to choose two words and identify the different ways they might use the words in and out of school.

Teach

Focus on the Big Question Ask the Article BQ, "What makes a good leader?" Students will answer this question after reading.

- *Connect to the Unit Big Question* Write the Unit and Article BQs on the board. Ask students to define what a leader is. Write key words from the responses.

Preread the Article Before students read, model how to preview and predict:

> **THINK ALOUD** *I see a photo with a caption and a box with a quotation in it. The photo shows a Duke basketball player and a man who looks like a coach. The caption says the coach is Mike Kryzyzewski. Maybe the article is about him. I need to look at the other features, like the title, subheadings, and the boxed quotation, to see if that is the case.*

Have students write a prediction.

Conduct a Guided Reading Read the article to the students as they follow along. Pause after each section to monitor students' comprehension.

- Ask "5 Ws and an H" questions.
- Call on a volunteer to summarize the section.

Reflect on the Article After reading the article, review ideas introduced before or during reading.

- Have students refer to their charts from the Real-Life Connection. Ask students to compare their responses to leaders described in the article.
- Have students evaluate their predictions.

Practice and Apply

Discuss the Questions Gauge students' comprehension and help them develop critical reading skills. (Answer Key, p. 131)

Connect to the Big Question Use the Three-Column Chart to answer the BQ.

- Have students write the Article BQ on their organizers. Ask them to write the names of the three leaders in the columns.
- Have volunteers identify traits the leaders share. Then they can answer the BQ.

Assess

Play a game to informally assess student learning.

- Ask students to write one true and one false statement from the article on separate slips of paper.
- Place students in pairs. Randomly select and read statements aloud. Have each pair briefly discuss and then write T or F.
- Check students' responses and see which team got the most answers correct. Review any questions that students had trouble with.

Reach All Learners

Build Fluency Choose a section from the article for an Echo Read.

- Choose a section and read it aloud one sentence at a time, placing emphasis on expression and emotion.
- Have students chorally read each sentence after you, imitating your expression and intonation.

Use Small Groups Have small groups make a presentation about their favorite leader in the article.

- Place students into groups of four.
- Tell students they will give a speech about a person's accomplishments and leadership qualities.
- Have groups choose their favorite leader from the article and write a short oral presentation.
- Have each group deliver its presentation to the class. As a class, discuss similarities and differences in what students described.

Assist Students Having Difficulty If students struggle to compare and contrast the three leaders discussed in the article, work with them to compare and contrast two of them.

- Use a transparency to create a Venn Diagram.
- Choose two of the leaders from the article and model recording details about each person. After details are recorded, have students make observations about similarities and differences.

WRITING JOURNAL

Extend

Write About It Students will use a concept web and write a brief description of what it takes to be a leader.

- Read and discuss the Writing Prompt. (Journal, p. 168) Review the Writing Rubric. Encourage students to add more points to the rubric to guide their work.
- Model how to use the organizer.
- Students should use the Check It and Fix It Section and the Writing Checklist to revise and evaluate their work.

Teaching Tip Remind students that a transition is a word or phrase that joins paragraphs and shows how ideas are connected. List some common transitions on a piece of chart paper, such as *however, first, next, in addition, also,* and *finally.* Continue to add transitions to the list.

Vocabulary Workshop Students extend their thinking about the Word Bank words.

- Students work in pairs or small groups on the Define It organizer. (Journal, p. 170)
- Have students add words to the Your Choice box and their personal word bank.
- Use the Show You Know exercise to assess students' understanding.

Model finding unfamiliar words:

> **THINK ALOUD** *As I was reading the article, I saw some words that are unfamiliar. In the first paragraph, I saw the word* motivate. *I know it is something leaders do, and I have heard people talk about coaches motivating their teams. I want to add* motivate *to my personal word bank so that I can learn it and use it correctly.*

UNIT 6

Rebuilding Communities

PROGRAM RESOURCES

ANTHOLOGY pp. 184–187

TEACHING GUIDE AND RESOURCES
- T-Chart **p. 151**
- Two-Column Journal **p. 153**
- Answer Key **p. 131**

REAL WORLD WRITING JOURNAL pp. 172–175

ANTHOLOGY

Preteach

Activate Prior Knowledge Have students copy and complete the chart in the Real-Life Connection. Students will revisit answers after they read.

Build Background *In addition to hurricanes, tornadoes, and fires, the United States also experiences earthquakes, floods, and heat waves that destroy property and claim lives. Other parts of the world also suffer from deadly and damaging natural disasters that are uncommon in the United States, including tsunamis and erupting volcanoes.*

Introduce Vocabulary

- Provide each student with a T-Chart. Have students label columns "Nouns" and "Verbs."
- Tell students to scan the article for boldface words and use context clues to help them place the words in the correct column.
- *Build Academic Vocabulary* Work with students to identify academic vocabulary in the Word Bank. Ask how they might use *community, culture, unify,* or *persuade* in social studies class.

Teach

Focus on the Big Question Ask the Article BQ, "What does it take to make a community unite and rebuild?" Students will answer this question after reading.

- *Connect to the Unit Big Question* Write the Unit and Article BQs on the board. Ask students whether they think the article will be more about individuals or communities.

Preread the Article Before students read, have them preview the article by skimming and scanning:

THINK ALOUD *You can quickly read, or skim, the article to get an idea of what you are going to read about. When you skim an article, you do not read each word. You try to understand the article's big ideas.*

Have students skim the title, subheadings, photo captions, and first sentences of paragraphs. Then ask them to write questions about the article.

Conduct a Guided Reading Read the article to students as they follow along. Pause after each section to monitor students' comprehension.

- Ask literal comprehension questions about each section, such as *What happened? When did it happen?*
- Follow up with inferential questions, such as *How did people probably feel? Why did they respond in these ways?*

Reflect on the Article After reading the article, review ideas introduced before or during reading.

- Have students revisit their knowledge ratings from the Real-Life Connection. Ask students what changed.
- Have students answer the questions they wrote while previewing the article.

Practice and Apply

Discuss the Questions Gauge students' comprehension and help them develop critical reading skills. (Answer Key, p. 131)

Connect to the Big Question Refocus students' attention on the Article BQ.

- Write the Article BQ on the board. As a class, discuss the question. Have students look for ideas in the article.
- Have students use the class notes to write a response to the BQ.

Assess

Have students complete the Two-Column Journal for you to informally assess.

- Provide each student with a copy of the organizer.
- Tell students that the left column should contain at least three natural disasters discussed in the article.
- Have students respond with their thoughts.

Reach All Learners

Build Fluency Choose a section from the article for a Paired Reading.

- Pair students and have them read silently.
- Direct one student to read aloud while the other follows along making notes.
- The listener provides suggestions and feedback. Students then reverse roles.

Use Small Groups Have students respond as a group to question five in the Use Clues section by creating an emergency plan.

- Assign groups of four students one of the three types of disasters.
- Have students write a plan for how they would help the community recover. Plans should address the specific disaster and use ideas from the article.
- Have each group share its plan in a class discussion.

Assist Students Having Difficulty If students struggle with inferential comprehension of the article, provide them with an outline of the article for taking notes.

- Review the facts that are stated in the article.
- Explain that sometimes authors do not tell us everything we need to know. We have to use the information to make inferences.
- Model making inferences and adding those to the outline.

WRITING JOURNAL

Extend

Write About It Students will use chart to plan and write an inspiring speech about rebuilding after a natural disaster.

- Read and discuss the Writing Prompt. (Journal, p. 172) Review the Writing Rubric. Encourage students to add more points to the rubric to guide their work.
- Model how to use the organizer.
- Students should use the Check It and Fix It Section and the Writing Checklist to revise and evaluate their work.

Model planning for writing by thinking aloud:

> **THINK ALOUD** *This speech is supposed to inspire people to take action and help others. Inspiring others means I have to get people excited to do something. I am going to include strong words, like "It is important that you help," and give examples that will touch people. This will help me make my speech inspiring.*

Vocabulary Workshop Students extend their thinking about the Word Bank words.

- Students work in pairs or small groups on the Define It organizer. (Journal, p. 174)
- Have students add words to the Your Choice box and to their personal word banks.
- Use the Show You Know exercise to assess students' understanding.

Teaching Tip Visual learners may find it easier to draw pictures illustrating a real-life example or their connection to the Word Bank words.

The Irresistible Urban Myth

PROGRAM RESOURCES

ANTHOLOGY pp. 188–191

TEACHING GUIDE AND RESOURCES
- K-W-L Chart **p. 145**
- Answer Key **p. 132**

REAL WORLD WRITING JOURNAL pp. 176–179

ANTHOLOGY

Preteach

Activate Prior Knowledge Have students copy and complete the web in the Real-Life Connection. Students will revisit answers after they read.

Build Background *Urban myths do not have to be set in cities or urban areas. The name "urban myth" separates today's myths from older ones. Modern technology helps these myths spread. Today there are many Web sites that are devoted to exposing the truth about different urban myths.*

Introduce Vocabulary

- Write the Word Bank words and their definitions in two columns in random order on the board.
- Have students scan the article for the boldface words. Have them use context clues to match the words with their definitions on the board.
- *Build Academic Vocabulary* Ask students how they might use the words *common*, *tradition*, and *unique* to describe an historical or current event.

Teach

Focus on the Big Question Ask the Article BQ, "What purposes do urban myths serve?" Students will answer this question after reading.

- *Connect to the Unit Big Question* Write the Unit and Article BQs on the board. Ask students to discuss how understanding urban myths might help them answer the Unit BQ.

Preread the Article Before students read, have them preview the title and first paragraph.

- Distribute copies of the K-W-L Chart.
- Direct students to fill out the first and second columns.
- Tell students they will fill out the third column as they read the article.

Conduct a Guided Reading Read the article to students as they follow along. Pause after each section to monitor students' comprehension.

- Survey students about whether they have heard any of the myths in the section.
- Model completing the third column of the K-W-L Chart:

> **THINK ALOUD** *The first section of the article gives a lot of background on urban myths. The main idea is that myths have been around a long time, and that urban myths reflect the fears and concerns of our time. I will add that information to the "What I Learned" column.*

Reflect on the Article After reading the article, review ideas introduced before or during reading.

- Have students add to their webs from the Real-Life Connection.
- Ask students whether they found the answers to questions they wrote in their charts.

Practice and Apply

Discuss the Questions Gauge students' comprehension and help them develop critical reading skills. (Answer Key, p. 132)

Connect to the Big Question Refocus students' attention on the Article BQ. Write the question on the board.

- Draw a Three-Column Chart on the board and label the columns *Myth*, *Type*, and *Purpose*.
- Have students list specific myths in the first column and identify the type in the second.
- Complete the third column. Have students consider what all the myths have in common and write a response to the Article BQ.

Assess

Informally assess students' understanding by having them write a definition and example of the following:

- a cautionary tale
- a shocking urban myth
- a sympathy scam
- a funny urban myth

Reach All Learners

Build Fluency Have students work in pairs to perform a dramatic reading.

- Choose sections of the article that describe urban myths—scary, funny, or sympathetic.
- Model reading a section using exaggerated emotion for dramatic effect.
- Direct students to take turns reading dramatically to one another with the listener providing feedback. Have students reverse roles.

Use Small Groups Engage students with a Write-Around activity.

- In groups of four, have each student begin with a piece of paper with the Article BQ written across the top.
- Have students write a response for one minute and then pass their papers to the right. The one-minute writing begins again, and students add to the paper in front of them responding to the idea that is already there.
- Continue until all students have written on each paper. Discuss with the class.

Assist Students Having Difficulty If students struggle to keep track of the main ideas in the article, provide them with a skeleton outline for taking notes.

- The outline should include the article title and any subheads with space for notes.
- Allow time after reading the article to go over the outline using an overhead transparency.
- Ask: *What questions do you still have?*
- Ask: *What was the point of today's lesson?*

WRITING JOURNAL

Extend

Write About It Students will use a Three-Column Chart to plan and write a welcome note for a Web site.

- Read and discuss the Writing Prompt. (Journal, p. 176) Review the Writing Rubric. Encourage students to add more points to the rubric to guide their work.
- Model how to use the organizer.
- Students should use the Check It and Fix It Section and the Writing Checklist to revise and evaluate their work.

Teaching Tip Remind students that their assignment is to write for a Web site. Have them brainstorm differences between print and online materials. Have students suggest design elements, graphics, or illustrations they would include on the Web site's welcome screen.

Vocabulary Workshop Students extend their thinking about the Word Bank words.

- Students work in pairs or small groups on the Define It organizer. (Journal, p. 178)
- Have students add words to the Your Choice box and their personal word bank.
- Use the Show You Know exercise to assess students' understanding.

Model completing the Define It chart:

> **THINK ALOUD** *To tell what the word common is, I will think about how I use the word. I know that it means when something happens a lot. I will put that in the chart. I know it also means the opposite of rare. So it does not mean something that happens only once. I will add that to the organizer, too.*

UNIT 6

The Ripple Effect

PROGRAM RESOURCES

ANTHOLOGY pp. 192–195

TEACHING GUIDE AND RESOURCES
- Web Map **p. 156**
- Series of Events Map **p. 150**
- Answer Key **p. 132**

REAL WORLD WRITING JOURNAL pp. 180–183

ANTHOLOGY

Preteach

Activate Prior Knowledge Have students copy and complete the chart in the Real-Life Connection. Students will revisit answers after they read.

Build Background *Many American high schools require seniors to complete a number of community service hours or to participate in "service learning," a combination of community service and instruction, in order to graduate. These requirements are designed to involve students with their communities.*

Introduce Vocabulary

- Read aloud the sentences from the article in which boldface vocabulary words appear. Discuss what each word means in context.
- Give students the opportunity to practice the vocabulary words in a new context.
- *Build Academic Vocabulary* Have students write *diversity, environment,* or *individual* in the center of a Web Map and fill in the outer circles with different ways the words can be used in school. Model completing the Web Map:

> **THINK ALOUD** *I have heard diversity in different classes. In science, we talked about the diversity of animals in a pond. In history class, we talked about how immigrants have created diversity in the United States.*

Teach

Focus on the Big Question Ask the Article BQ, "Do small, individual efforts really matter, or must large, group efforts be made for real change to occur?" Students will answer this question after reading.

- *Connect to the Unit Big Question* Write the Unit and Article BQs on the board. Have students use different colors of chalk to circle related words in each question.

Preread the Article Have students preview the article's features and predict.

- Ask students to read the title, headings, and photo captions.
- Have students write a prediction about how the information in the article is organized.

Conduct a Guided Reading Read the article to students as they follow along. Pause after each section to monitor students' comprehension.

- Ask students questions about each section that help them make personal connections, such as *Do you know someone who helped change a community?*
- Call on volunteers to share their thoughts.

Reflect on the Article After reading the article, review ideas introduced before or during reading.

- Have students add the two examples from the article to their Real-Life Connection charts.
- Ask students whether their predictions about the article's organization were correct.

Practice and Apply

Discuss the Questions Gauge students' comprehension and help them develop critical reading skills. (Answer Key, p. 132)

Connect to the Big Question Use the Series of Events Map to answer the BQ.

- Have students write the Article BQ on their organizers. In the first box, have students write the problems that either Jennica Jenkins or Jennifer Staple saw. Have students add events to their organizers.
- Call for volunteers to answer the BQ.

Assess

Have students create a Learning Log for you to informally assess. Students should answer these questions:

- What did you do in class today? What organizations did you learn about?
- What did you find interesting?
- Would your community benefit from these programs? Why or why not?

Reach All Learners

Build Fluency Choose a section from the article for an Echo Reading.

- Read the section one sentence at a time, emphasizing grouping words into phrases.
- Have students echo read the sentence after you, imitating your phrasing.

Use Small Groups Have small groups collaborate to create a proposal for changing the community.

- In groups of four, have students identify a problem.
- In their proposals, students should suggest whether the problem is best addressed by an individual, a group, or a combination of the two.
- Have groups share their proposals with the class.

Assist Students Having Difficulty If students struggle to understand the order of events in the article, work with them to establish sequence.

- Review the ripple analogy with students.
- Ask students to identify the situations that caused the people in the article to start a ripple. Have students explain how the ripple got larger and larger. Model completing the Series of Events Map as a transparency.

WRITING JOURNAL

Extend

Write About It Students will use a graphic organizer to plan and write an introduction to a photo exhibit.

- Read and discuss the Writing Prompt. (Journal, p. 180) Review the Writing Rubric. Encourage students to add more points to the rubric to guide their work.
- Model how to use the organizer.
- Students should use the Check It and Fix It Section and the Writing Checklist to revise and evaluate their work.

Model revising by thinking aloud:

> **THINK ALOUD** *Now that I am done with my draft, I need to reread it to make sure it makes sense. First I am going to check that I underlined my opinion. Next I want to make sure that I included information from the article to support my opinion. I am also going to put a check mark next to my Word Bank words to make sure I used at least one. Finally, I am going to see if I can find any grammar mistakes to fix.*

Vocabulary Workshop Students extend their thinking about the Word Bank words.

- Students work in pairs or small groups on the Define It organizer. (Journal, p. 182)
- Have students add words to the Your Choice box and to their personal word banks.
- Use the Show You Know exercise to assess students' understanding.

Teaching Tip Compile a class list of the words students wrote for the Your Choice activity. Discuss the words that appeared most frequently on the list. Review different ways for students to learn new words, such as drawing pictures, identifying synonyms and antonyms, and using the words in a sentence.

Trickster Appeal Revealed!

PROGRAM RESOURCES

ANTHOLOGY pp. 196–199

TEACHING GUIDE AND RESOURCES
- Two-Column Journal p. 153
- Comic Strip Organizer p. 141
- Answer Key p. 132

REAL WORLD WRITING JOURNAL pp. 184–187

ANTHOLOGY

Preteach

Activate Prior Knowledge Take a class survey of *agree* or *disagree* for each statement in the Real-Life Connection. Students will revisit answers after they read.

Build Background *A folktale is a traditional story, usually with an unknown author, that was often passed down by retelling. A myth is a traditional story that usually explains the history of a group of people. Not all folktales and myths include tricksters.*

Introduce Vocabulary

- Read the Word Bank words and definitions with students.
- Ask students to see how many of the words they can use in a single sentence.
- *Build Academic Vocabulary* Have students write two to three sentences explaining how *argue, culture,* or *unique* might be used in social studies or health classes.

Teach

Focus on the Big Question Ask the Article BQ, "What makes trickster characters so appealing?" Students will answer this question after reading.

- *Connect to the Unit Big Question* Write the Unit and Article BQs on the board. Ask students how they think a trickster might be connected to the ideas of *community* and *individual.*

Preread the Article Before students read, model how to preview and predict:

> **THINK ALOUD** *The first subheading says "Tricky, Slick, and Sly." I think these might be words that describe tricksters. When I read that section of the article, I will see if* tricky, slick, *and* sly *apply to tricksters. That will help me understand tricksters better and know what they are like.*

Have students read the remaining subheads and write a prediction about each section.

Conduct a Guided Reading Read the article to students as they follow along. Pause after each section to monitor students' comprehension.

- Call on volunteers to summarize what they learned in each section.
- Ask what they learned about tricksters.

Reflect on the Article After reading the article, review ideas introduced before or during reading.

- Retake the poll from the Real-Life Connection. Have answers changed? Why?
- Ask students whether they correctly predicted what each section of the article was about.

Practice and Apply

Discuss the Questions Gauge students' comprehension and help them develop critical reading skills. (Answer Key, p. 132)

Connect to the Big Question Have students use the Two-Column Journal to answer the BQ.

- Have students write the Article BQ at the top of their organizers. Have them list characteristics of tricksters in the left column. Have students evaluate what they read and write their thoughts in the right column.
- Call for volunteers to answer the BQ.

Assess

Have students create a trickster comic strip to show their understanding of the article.

- Tell students to create a trickster character and story using what they learned from the article.
- Have students use words and pictures to tell their stories.

Assess comic strips for understanding.

Reach All Learners

Build Fluency Choose a section from the article for a Paired Reading.

- Pair students and have them read silently.
- Direct one student to read aloud while the other follows along making notes.
- The listener provides suggestions and feedback. Students then reverse roles.

Use Small Groups Engage students with a Write-Around activity.

- In groups of four, have each student begin with a piece of paper with the Article BQ written across the top.
- Have students write a response for one minute and then pass their papers to the right. The one-minute writing begins again, and students add to the paper in front of them responding to the idea that is already there.
- Continue until all students have written on each paper. Discuss with the class.

Assist Students Having Difficulty If students struggle to make connections between the Article and Unit BQ, have them apply background knowledge.

- Ask students to describe tricksters they know or that are described in the article. Point out that these tricksters are all individuals.
- Ask students what kind of relationships tricksters have with groups, such as their families, schools, and communities.
- Have students make connections by asking them whether a trickster is more interested in himself or in the community, and to explain why.

WRITING JOURNAL

Extend

Write About It Students will use a graphic organizer to plan and write a short chapter on tricksters.

- Read and discuss the Writing Prompt. (Journal, p. 184) Review the Writing Rubric. Encourage students to add more points to the rubric to guide their work.
- Model how to use the organizer.
- Students should use the Check It and Fix It Section and the Writing Checklist to revise and evaluate their work.

Teaching Tip Help students brainstorm examples of tricksters from the article as well as others that they know of. Remind students that not all cartoon characters are tricksters. Tell them to make sure their examples fit the definition and are appropriate for the topic.

Vocabulary Workshop Students extend their thinking about the Word Bank words.

- Students work in pairs or small groups on the Define It organizer. (Journal, p. 186)
- Have students add words to the Your Choice box and to their personal word banks.
- Use the Show You Know exercise to assess students' understanding.

Model completing the Word Play activity:

| THINK ALOUD | *I know that the Word Bank word* custom *means something people do regularly. I have heard the word used to describe something families do, like having a big meal on Sundays. Some words that have a similar meaning to* custom *might be* habit *or* tradition. *I can find these words by looking in a thesaurus. I am going see which word makes the most sense in the sentence.* |

Community or individual—which is more important?

Introduce the Unit Project

Interview Students will conduct interviews and work with partners to answer the Big Question: *Community or individual—which is more important?*

- Read through the steps of the assignment with students.
- Point out the rubric so that students will know their goals for the assignment. Add other rubric points with students to guide their work.
- Allow time for students to practice their interview. Encourage listeners to offer their feedback and advice on the questions and answers.

Model Model how to strengthen the interview by thinking aloud.

| THINK ALOUD | *At the end of the interview I am going to summarize how my partner answered the Big Question.* My partner believes that individuals are more important. My partner believes this because… During my interview, my partner said… *That way, the audience will be able to follow my ideas.* |

Teaching Tip Explain to students that when reporters interview someone, they often use a tape recorder to get the person's exact words. Have students incorporate at least one direct quotation from their partners in their summaries. Review how to punctuate quotations.

Conclude the Unit

Review Unit Objectives Return to the unit objectives and ask students to evaluate how well they mastered each one on a scale of 1 to 5, with 1 being low and 5 being high. Discuss how lower scores could be improved.

Reflect on the Learning Examine the unit chart with students. Ask them to reflect on what they have learned. They can write or discuss with the class or in small groups. Ask questions such as:

- What was the most interesting article you read? What did you like about it?

- How did your ideas about individuals and communities change as you read through the articles?
- Which topic would you like to know more about? What do you still wonder about it?
- How did the writing assignments and the interview help you form your ideas about whether communities or individuals are more important?
- What connections can you make between the ideas in this article and your own life? How might these experiences help you understand the role of individuals and communities?

Name _____

Word Bank Quiz

WORD LIST A			
common	duty	group	tradition
community	environment	individual	unify
diversity	family	persuade	voice

Ten of the unit Word Bank words are defined in parentheses in the article below. As you read the article, use Word List A, above, to figure out which word best fits each definition. Write the word on the line provided. (You will not use every word on the list.) Then go on to the next page of the quiz.

Cleaning Up Our Parks

In my **(1. group of people living in the same area)** _____,

people have a **(2. meaningful belief or habit)** _____. One Sunday

afternoon each month, people gather in the park alongside the lake. We clean up the

trash and do other things to improve the **(3. surroundings)** _____.

Some people believe it is everyone's **(4. way of behaving required by a person's sense**

of what is right) _____ to improve our town. Other people believe

doing this service work helps to **(5. bring together)** _____ the

people who live here.

The monthly cleanup projects were started by a young **(6. one person)**

_____, a high school student. While she was playing fetch in the lake

with her dog, the dog became tangled in garbage in the water. She worried what might have

happened if she had not been there. That evening, when she told her **(7. group of related**

people) _____ what had happened, they urged her to **(8. speak one's**

mind) _____ her concerns to town officials. Instead she decided to

(9. convince) _____ a **(10. individuals who have things in common)**

_____ of fellow students to join her in taking action.

UNIT 6 Word Bank Quiz

WORD LIST B			
argue	culture	duty	team
common	custom	environment	unique
completely	diversity	ethnicity	various

Ten more Word Bank words are defined in parentheses in the rest of the
article, below. As you read the article, use Word List B, above, to figure out
which word best fits each definition. Write the word on the line provided.
(You will not use every word on the list.)

_____

The student was creative in getting people to help. She asked **(11. different kinds of)**

_____ student groups to help out. They turned the cleanups into

a **(12. group working toward the same goal)** _____ competition

to see who could collect the most trash. Soon other groups like churches and exercise

clubs joined in the cleanup, creating **(13. many different kinds of people or things)**

_____ in the people who volunteered. Most of the trash collected is

(14. ordinary or easily found) _____ items, like aluminum cans and

paper wrappers. However, **(15. one of a kind)** _____ items are also

found, including single shoes and even a surfboard! It soon became a **(16. action done

regularly)** _____ for the person finding the most unusual item to

win a prize: the money collected from recycling aluminum cans.

Some people **(17. give reasons for or against an idea)** _____

that the city, not volunteers, should be cleaning the parks. Our park is not **(18. fully)**

_____ clean, but we have created a **(19. set of beliefs and habits

that form a way of life)** _____ in our city that takes pride in how

our town looks. The actions of one concerned teenager brought a wide variety of people

together—people of every age, race, faith, and **(20. background shared with similar

people)** _____—in the spirit of giving and improving our town.

When Animals Help People

Real-Life Connection, p. 4
1. True
2. True
3. True
4. False

Wrap It Up, Anthology, p. 7
1. A therapy animal is an animal that works with people, providing help and support.
2. Therapy animals can help patients in hospitals and nursing homes, they can help students in school, and they can help people with disabilities.
3. Swimming with dolphins can help people with disabilities by helping them to feel happy and free.
4. Sample response: One way to test whether reading to an animal can help kids learn to read would be to compare two groups of kids. One group would read to animals and the other group would read alone or to a teacher. Then, both groups could be tested on their reading ability.
5. Sample response: Living on a horse ranch could help teens learn responsibility because there are a lot of jobs to do on a horse ranch. Pitching in and doing chores and caring for the animals would help teens learn to be more responsible.
6. Sample response: I do not think dolphins should be used as therapy animals, because it is not fair to the animals. Dolphins are sometimes upset by the presence of people in their tanks, and they prefer to be swimming in the ocean.

Connect to the Big Question
Sample response: I think working with people helps some animals but harms others. Animals that are already social and domesticated, like dogs and horses, benefit from the love they receive when they work with people. However, animals that are happier in the wild could be harmed by working with people.

Vocabulary Exercise, Writing Journal, p. 5
My sister and I read every day. We love <u>reading</u>. I hope my little brother learns to read soon. I am <u>hoping</u> that he will enjoy reading, too. Right now, he loves to play. He is such a <u>playful</u> kid! My mom says <u>playing</u> is a kid's job.

Learning the Truth in China

Wrap It Up, Anthology, p. 11
1. The word *google* means "to search for information."
2. The key words *democracy, freedom, justice*, and *human rights* are frequently blocked by Chinese censors. The government blocks these sites so no one can see them.
3. Some U.S. companies block information, because it is the only way for them to do business in China.
4. Sample response: The Chinese government probably uses cartoon characters to help police the Internet because it makes the government appear friendlier and less threatening and oppressive.
5. Sample response: I think efforts to open up the Internet in China will be successful if the government changes its policies. However, for now I think the Internet will continue to be censored because China is not yet a democracy.
6. Sample response: Based on this article, it does seem that Chinese students are more motivated to get information than students in other countries. Students in the United States can search freely. Chinese students, who cannot, work harder to get around censors and find the information they want.

Connect to the Big Question
Sample response: The country in which you live has a big impact on the information you can find. In countries like China, the government controls the information. The government gets to decide who reads what. In countries like the United States, people have the freedom to search for and find the information they want.

Vocabulary Exercise, Writing Journal, p. 9
Kim is also a great football player. No one can run faster than he does, and that <u>quickness</u> makes him a good receiver. Moreover, his <u>toughness</u> enables him to get tackled without getting hurt. I will feel great <u>sadness</u> when he graduates this spring and leaves our middle school.

In the Grip of Graffiti

Wrap It Up, Anthology, p. 15
1. Tagging is spray painting your nickname on public property.

2. Graffiti sometimes covers street signs or subway trains. Families have to pay to have graffiti removed from their property, and cities have to pay to clean up graffiti on bridges, tunnels, and statues.

3. Graffiti can be used to spread ideas about politics, life, or society. Some people think graffiti is a good way to show off talent, and others believe that graffiti adds personality to a neighborhood or city.

4. Sample response: A store in an area free of graffiti might do more business than a store covered in graffiti because the graffiti could scare customers away. People might think the store was in a dangerous area.

5. Sample response: I would advise cities that want to stop graffiti to enforce stricter punishments for taggers and make them clean up the graffiti themselves.

6. Sample response: I think graffiti looks cool, but it should be used for art murals and exhibits that are approved. Taggers should not destroy property just because they want to spray paint.

Connect to the Big Question

Sample response: The article did not make me change my mind. I think graffiti is more of a problem than an art form. However, the article did make me think about the amount of money a city has to spend to remove graffiti and how it is really everyone's problem because it is a community problem.

Vocabulary Exercise, Writing Journal, p. 13

1. enjoyable
2. comfortable
3. breakable

Cross Your Fingers!

Wrap It Up, Anthology, p. 19

1. *Superstitians* were soldiers in ancient Rome who lived through battle. It means "those standing above."

2. Three things that supposedly bring bad luck are a black cat, walking under a ladder, and forgetting to say "Bless you" to someone who sneezes.

3. Rabbits became a sign of good luck because there were so many of them in the spring and people had plenty to eat. Therefore, rabbits became a sign of good health.

4. Sample response: I think people are still superstitious because it comforts people to think they can control the outcome of events or prevent bad luck.

5. Sample response: It would be hard to prove whether a superstition is true or false, but you could test the reliability of a lucky object. You could pick up a lucky penny and then pay close attention to whether or not anything lucky actually happened that same day.

6. Sample response: Yes, believing you are lucky can help you succeed because if you have a positive attitude you are likely to try harder, and hard work is usually rewarded with success.

Connect to the Big Question

Sample response: I don't think there is any real truth to superstitions, although the stories behind them can be interesting. I think superstitions are only true to the person who believes in their power.

Vocabulary Workshop, Writing Journal, p. 17

1. unhealthy
2. unlucky
3. unnatural
4. unbelievable

The Word on Bullies

Wrap It Up, Anthology, p. 23

1. Hitting or pushing someone are two examples of physical bullying.

2. Two other kinds of bullying are verbal bullying and relationship bullying.

3. If someone tried to bully me, I could speak up for myself or tell an adult.

4. Sample response: People sometimes think bullies are tough and confident because bullies seem tough when they pick on others.

5. Sample response: If I were the school principal, I would have a conference with the bully and his or her parents. I would also make sure the school had a strong policy against bullying so that all kids knew that bullying would be taken seriously.

6. Sample response: I do think the article gives good advice about how to stop bullies because there are several suggestions, and three of them are things kids can do on their own. Not all kids like to tell an adult right away, so it is good to know that there are ways you can handle a bully yourself.

Connect to the Big Question

Sample response: The real truth about bullies is that they are cowards. Frequently, bullies pick on others because they feel badly about themselves, and putting someone else down makes them feel better.

Campers Give Peace a Chance

Wrap It Up, Anthology, p. 27

1. A peace camp is a camp where kids from war-torn countries go.
2. Young people play games, do activities, and learn understanding and respect for people who are different from them at peace camp.
3. Campers fear each other before they even meet because at home they don't know anyone from the other side of the conflict and they have heard scary stories about the other side.
4. Sample response: The lessons that kids at peace camp learn could help kids in the United States by teaching them to respect others with different traditions and cultures.
5. Sample response: I think sports helps people understand each other because when you work together on a team you don't think about how your team member is different from you. Players are focused on winning, and that helps them to forget their differences.
6. Sample response: I think kids in the United States could really benefit from attending peace camps. I think kids would like to attend for the sports and the activities, but also to meet and learn about people who are different from them. It could help kids in the United States get along.

Connect to the Big Question

Sample response: I think the best way to understand people who are different is to get to know people who are different. When you get to know people who are different, you are more likely to understand that people have a lot in common. It can also help a person realize that what they thought about another person or group of people was not true.

Vocabulary Exercise, Writing Journal, p. 25

1. imagination
2. communication
3. information
4. Answers will vary.

Return to Humanity

Wrap It Up, Anthology, p. 31

1. Ishmael Beah was 12 when war broke out in his country.
2. Beah ended up as a soldier because he was captured by the government's army.
3. War caused society in Sierra Leone to fall apart. Kids did not go to school, people were killed, and kids were forced to become soldiers.
4. Sample response: Even many years after they have stopped fighting, child soldiers carry emotional scars. War changes child soldiers because after fighting they live with fear, anxiety, and hopelessness.
5. Sample response: Former child soldiers who try to ignore their past might never return to a normal life. They need help and support in order to recover.
6. Sample response: I think the worst thing about being a refugee would be the fear of being killed or captured and forced to fight.

Connect to the Big Question

Sample response: I think events in a person's life do shape who they are. However, people do not have to let bad events, such as being a child soldier, ruin their whole lives. People can take steps to move past negative events in their lives to grow and learn and to help them become stronger.

Vocabulary Exercise, Writing Journal, p. 29

1. imaginative
2. competitive
3. deceptive

Luol Deng: A True Winner

Wrap It Up, Anthology, p. 35

1. Luol Deng and his family left Sudan because the country was at war.
2. Mosquito nets protect Sudanese refugees from malaria.
3. After he moved to the United States, Deng attended high school and played basketball.
4. Sample response: Deng probably remembers what it was like to live in Sudan. He knows it is a hard life for the refugees and wants to help his fellow countrymen and women.

5. Sample response: I would say that it is important to help people in refugee camps, because they have been driven out of their own countries and are in need of assistance.

6. Sample response: Yes, athletes should look to Deng as a role model, because athletes have a lot of advantages. If they all pitched in and helped others, they could do a lot of good.

Connect to the Big Question

Sample response: Deng's past definitely made him the person he is today. He remembers what it is like to have to flee a country at war, and he knows the fears of refugees and what life is like in Sudan. Without these experiences, he may not have helped the people of Sudan and would not be the person he is today.

Vocabulary Exercise, Writing Journal, p. 33

1. repeatedly
2. supposedly
3. contentedly

Word Bank Quiz

1. consequence
2. reveal
3. debate
4. evidence
5. factual
6. reality
7. explain
8. affect
9. awareness
10. convince
11. rarely
12. conclude
13. evaluate
14. perceive
15. believable
16. observe
17. pattern
18. mean
19. view
20. insight

Answer Key

Athletes as Role Models

Wrap It Up, Anthology, p. 43

1. Dikembe Mutombo is a man from the Congo. He is a star basketball player.
2. Dikembe Mutombo gives people in Congo medicine, and he is building a hospital there.
3. Sammy Sosa used a corked bat during a game.
4. Sample response: Corked bats make the ball go farther. They are also easier to swing. That is unfair to players who do not use corked bats.
5. Sample response: Yes, too many parents do not tell their children how to act. They even act badly themselves. Children learn more from their parents than from anyone else.
6. Sample response: I would pick athletes who gave a lot of money to help people and who were very kind to people.

Connect to the Big Question

Sample response: Athletes should be good role models because a lot of children look up to athletes and act like athletes.

Vocabulary Exercise, Writing Journal, p. 39

1. to bring shame on
2. to not like
3. stop

Coyotes on the Go

Wrap It Up, Anthology, p. 47

1. A coyote is an animal that is a member of the dog family.
2. Coyotes are very adaptable. They will eat almost anything.
3. Pioneers cut down forests and killed wolves. That meant there were more coyotes. Then people began building houses and cities where the coyotes lived.
4. Sample response: If people feed coyotes, the coyotes will think that people will always give them food. Then coyotes might attack people who don't give them food.
5. Sample response: I would tell people not to leave their pets alone outside. I would also cover my trashcans.
6. Sample response: Coyotes are enemies to people because they will hurt people and their pets.

Connect to the Big Question

Sample Response: Coyotes are winners because they can adapt and live anywhere.

Vocabulary Exercise, Writing Journal, p. 43

1. to make into a law
2. to make slaves of
3. to give power to

Moms and Dads in the Military?

Wrap It Up, Anthology, p. 51

1. The Sullivan brothers were five brothers who joined the Navy during World War II. They all served on the same ship.
2. They all died when their ship went down at sea.
3. A serviceman or service woman who is the only child left in a family may be removed from a war zone if two or more of the soldier's siblings were killed while serving in the navy, marine corps, or coast guard.
4. The military does not think a new law is needed. Some military leaders think that the problem of two parents being sent to a war zone at the same time does not happen often.
5. Sample Response: There would be a lot fewer people in the military if parents could not join.
6. Sample Response: The military should pay for child care because people in the military put their lives on the line.

Connect to the Big Question

Sample Response: The military should pay a relative to come and take care of the children.

Vocabulary Exercise, Writing Journal, p. 47

Word in Sentence	Meaning 1	Meaning 2
The teacher said they had to **face** the fact that studying was the only way to learn.	front of the head, which features the eyes, nose, and mouth	to accept something to be true
Marta could easily **picture** the warm days of summer.	a photograph	to imagine something
Olivia knew that growing up would be a **sum** of good and bad days.	the total amount of something	to add up a series of numbers

Sports Parents

Wrap It Up, Anthology, p. 55

1. Mary Pierce was a tennis player. Her father was her manager.
2. Sports is good exercise. Sports teaches teamwork. Sports teaches people how to perform well under pressure.
3. Mary Pierce's father behaved badly. Cal Ripken, Sr., behaved well.
4. Sample response: Many parents think that pushing their children to compete and win is good for them. They also want to see their children win.
5. Sample response: Teammates need to communicate well because they have to act together.
6. Sample response: No, the most important reason for children to play sports is to get exercise. There are too many children who are obese and unhealthy.

Connect to the Big Question

Sample response: When parents put too much pressure on kids to succeed at sports, kids begin to feel uncomfortable around their parents. They also begin to feel bad about the sport. They might not want to do it anymore, even though they are good at it.

Vocabulary Exercise, Writing Journal, p. 51

Prefix		Word		New Word	Meaning
mis	+	behave	=	misbehave	behave badly or wrongly
mis	+	trust	=	mistrust	to have no trust or confidence in
mis	+	fortune	=	misfortune	mishap or bad luck
mis	+	under-stand	=	misunderstand	to understand incorrectly

The Kindness of Kin

Real-Life Connection, Anthology, p. 57

1. False
2. True
3. False

Wrap It Up, Anthology, p. 59

1. A kinship parent is a substitute parent who is a relative.
2. 389,631 children in California are in kinship care.
3. Sample response: Amy's mom was not a good parent. Amy took care of her brothers and sisters. After all the children were taken away from the mom, Amy promised to take care of them. She went to court and became their foster parent.
4. Sample answer: A relative knows the child and knows the parent. A relative would understand what had happened.
5. They can go to kinship care programs.
6. Sample response: Yes, it was better to keep the family together. Also, Amy had shown that she could take care of her sisters and brothers.

Connect to the Big Question

Sample response: A problem with being a kinship parent is that you have to give up your own dreams. A reward is that you are doing something to help a member of your family.

Sister Champions

Wrap It Up, Anthology, p. 63

1. Venus and Serena Williams are sisters who are tennis stars.
2. They needed to concentrate on school.
3. Serena is a clothing designer and actor. Venus is a clothing designer and has an interior design company.
4. Sample response: She hates to see her sister lose.
5. Sample response: No matter what happens, you are my friend.
6. Sample response: I would say that I wasn't going to play.

Connect to the Big Question

Sample response: People can learn that you can play really hard against each other and still be friends. Winning and losing doesn't have to hurt a friendship.

Vocabulary Exercise, Writing Journal, p. 59

Prefix		Root		New Word	Word Meaning
op (means "against")	+	pos	=	oppose	to put against
ex (means "out")	+	pos	=	expose	to make known
inter (means "between")	+	pos	=	interpose	to intrude

Two Views of the Zoo

Wrap It Up, Anthology, p. 67

1. Endangered species are animals that are dying out and disappearing from the face of the earth.
2. The San Diego Wild Animal Park was really big. Cages were gone and animals had large stretches of land to explore.
3. Sample response: People in favor of zoos believe they help endangered species. They also feel zoos educate people about animals. People who don't like zoos say that animals have a right to their freedom. They say that the breeding programs don't work at zoos. They also say that people can learn about animals by watching movies about them.
4. Sample response: Animal rights groups would probably want zoos to have more space for animals and for zoos to be more like where animals would live in the wild.
5. Sample response: People would learn about animals from movies and animals would be happier.
6. Sample response: I would say they were wrong. I would ask that person, "How would you like to live in a small cage?"

Connect to the Big Question

Sample response: Yes, I used to love the zoo. I had thought that the animals were happy. But now I know that they may be bored and unhappy. That makes me sad.

Either Too Young or Too Old

Wrap It Up, Anthology, p. 71

1. A citizen has to be eighteen to vote.
2. Sample response: Teens can be tried as adults. Teens can have a job and pay taxes. Teens can drive cars.
3. Sample response: Some people do not want to retire because they are afraid they will be bored. Other people cannot afford to retire.
4. Sample response: A sixteen-year-old learns about the U.S. government in school. An older person may have forgotten what they learned about the U.S. government a long time ago.
5. Sample response: A person should know how the government works. A person should also know what is important in the election.
6. Sample response: Yes, I would vote because I want to make things better.

Connect to the Big Question

Sample response: There is no right age to vote or retire. Of course a three-year-old doesn't know enough to vote. But someone who is sixteen might know just as much as someone who is twenty. And a person should be able to work for as long as they want to, so long as they can still do the job.

Word Bank Quiz

1. competition
2. assume
3. desire
4. attitude
5. style
6. communication
7. understanding
8. prepare
9. challenge
10. obstacle
11. conflict
12. subject
13. compromise
14. misunderstanding
15. danger
16. plan
17. resolution
18. opposition
19. struggle
20. outcome

UNIT 3

Answer Key

Travel to Mars

Wrap It Up, Anthology, p. 79

1. It would take many months to get to Mars.
2. Nuclear energy could cut the trip to two months.
3. To live on Mars, we would have to solve the problems of extreme cold, lack of oxygen, and harmful cosmic rays.
4. Sample response: It is human nature to explore. Also, human beings might want to live on Mars someday.
5. Sample response: I would tell people traveling to Mars to take plenty of food and water with them.
6. Sample response: No, I would not go to Mars. It sounds uncomfortable and dangerous.

Connect to the Big Question

Sample response: Before people can live on Mars, we need to figure out how to get there quickly and solve the practical problems of staying alive.

Vocabulary Exercise, Writing Journal, p. 73

1. imperfect
2. impersonal
3. impractical
4. immature

Look Who's Talking

Wrap It Up, Anthology, p. 83

1. Boy topics are about things, and girl topics are about feelings.
2. Deborah Tannen believes that girls look down on others who stand out or try to appear better than others while boys use talking as a way to get attention.
3. Deborah Cameron believes that there is not much difference in the way girls and boys speak. She thinks we only find differences in their speaking styles because we expect to.
4. Sample response: Different speaking styles might make it difficult for boys and girls to understand each other.
5. Sample response: You might test the speaking-style theory by listening to a lot of conversations.

6. Sample response: I think Deborah Cameron's theory is correct because I know boys who are nice and polite and girls who are trying to get attention when they talk.

Connect to the Big Question

Sample response: I do not think we can learn much from differences in speaking styles because I do not believe that there really are any differences.

Vocabulary Exercise, Writing Journal, p. 77

1. to try out an idea
2. highest achievers
3. a string of words

Making Sport of Tradition

Real-Life Connection, p. 84

1. True
2. True
3. False
4. False

Wrap It Up, Anthology, p. 87

1. A mascot is a person or animal that represents a team.
2. About 4 million people identify themselves as Native American.
3. People who oppose the use of Native American names or mascots believe that their use by teams makes fun of Native American culture and values and makes all tribes look alike.
4. Sample response: Land developers want to build on ancient Native American burial grounds. Native Americans oppose this because they feel these grounds are sacred.
5. Sample response: Problems between Native Americans and others might be solved if each group learns about the other's needs and beliefs.
6. Sample response: I think the Native Americans are right. We do not have to develop all the land there is, and land developers could easily find other locations to build on.

Connect to the Big Question

Sample response: It think it is very important to learn about other people's cultures so that we can get along better.

Vocabulary Exercise, Writing Journal, p. 81

1. valuable
2. evaluation
3. value
4. invaluable

In Your Dreams

Wrap It Up, Anthology, p. 91

1. Dr. Garfield says we are creating images out of our emotions.
2. People used to think dreams were messages from the gods and could tell them about the future.
3. Sample response: Dreams are emotions and memories from our lives that our brains do not put in order for us.
4. Sample response: The teacher's dream about the speeding car shows her fears that a substitute teacher might teach difficult information to her students too quickly.
5. Sample response: People might be curious about dreams because they are so unusual and interesting.
6. Sample response: Yes, I think dreams might give us some clues to what we are feeling and worrying about.

Connect to the Big Question

Sample response: I think we might be able to learn some things about our own feelings from dreams.

Vocabulary Exercise, Writing Journal, p. 85

1. similarity
2. royalty
3. cruelty
4. loyalty

The Titans Remember

Wrap It Up, Anthology, p. 95

1. Coach Herman Boone is the man who coached the 1971 football team at T. C. Williams High School.
2. Someone threw a brick in the movie and a part of a toilet in real life.
3. Sample response: In real life not all of the teammates became friends. The movie also made up some people and exaggerated some events.
4. Sample response: The story teaches a really good lesson about life.

5. Sample response: I would ask him what made him decide to have the team train away from the school. I would also ask him if he knew he was going to get the team to work together when he started.
6. Sample response: No, I do not. I think it is important to tell the truth about history.

Connect to the Big Question

Sample response: I think people should learn about each other's cultures and spend time together.

Vocabulary Exercise, Writing Journal, p. 89

1. quarterback; football
2. teammate
3. filmmaker
4. schoolhouse

The Price of Discovery

Real-Life Connection, p. 96

1. No
2. Yes
3. Yes
4. No

Wrap It Up, Anthology, p. 99

1. On February 1, 2003, the Columbia shuttle broke apart before landing.
2. Most Americans were excited about the 1969 moon landing and supported exploration.
3. After 1971 NASA stopped American flights to the moon.
4. Sample response: The shuttle program is very expensive and not very exciting.
5. Sample response: We have a lot of very useful inventions that came from the space program. Also, we know more about the solar system and how humans might one day be able to live on other planets.
6. Sample response: Yes, I think we should keep exploring the moon because we could learn many more things about space.

Connect to the Big Question

Sample response: Yes, I think the space program is worth the cost because knowledge is very important. We may one day need to live on other planets. If we do not explore space, we will never learn about the universe around us.

Vocabulary Exercise, Writing Journal, p. 93

1. imagination
2. organization
3. examination
4. combination

Someone Has to Do It

Real-Life Connection, p. 100

1. True
2. True
3. True
4. False

Wrap It Up, Anthology, p. 103

1. People who fish have the most dangerous job in the United States.
2. Logging is dangerous because loggers can get killed by falling trees and branches.
3. Sample response: People do dangerous jobs because they cannot get other jobs, because their families have always done these jobs, because the jobs pay more, or because they want to work outside.
4. Sample response: The road is a dangerous workplace because people get in car and truck accidents.
5. Sample response: I would make trucking less dangerous by making sure people do not drive for too many hours without a break.
6. Sample response: No, I probably would not take one of the jobs in the article. I would rather have a safer job.

Connect to the Big Question

Sample response: I think we can learn from people who do dangerous jobs that there are a lot of decisions to make when you are thinking about a job.

Vocabulary Exercise, Writing Journal, p. 97

1. The loggers spent their day <u>cutting down trees</u> and <u>stacking logs.</u> *people who cut down trees or clear land of trees*
2. The <u>drivers</u> will transport the logs to <u>different places</u> including <u>distant countries.</u> *to move to a new place*
3. Because they work with <u>power lines that carry electricity,</u> electrical workers are <u>at risk</u> of being electrocuted. *shocked by electric current*

Have No Fear

Wrap It Up, Anthology, p. 107

1. Phobias are fears about things that probably will not hurt you.
2. Fear is normal and necessary because it warns you about dangerous things.
3. Sample response: Fear is a normal reaction to things that might harm you. A phobia is an abnormal fear of things that prevents you from doing things such as giving speeches or petting a friendly dog.
4. Sample response: Maybe taking small steps helps you get used to the thing you are afraid of.
5. Sample response: I might start by looking at pictures of horses, then go with a therapist to a horse farm and look at them from far away.
6. Sample response: It might be important to get over a phobia because you might have to be around something you are afraid of and it would make your life hard.

Connect to the Big Question

Sample response: First, I would not make fun of them or tell them they are silly. Then I might tell them to go to a therapist to get help.

Vocabulary Exercise, Writing Journal, p. 101

1. accidental
2. environmental
3. electrical
4. industrial

Word Bank Quiz

1. understand
2. discover
3. examine
4. analyze
5. information
6. approach
7. background
8. discipline
9. curiosity
10. organize
11. topic
12. explore
13. facts
14. possible
15. investigate
16. inquire
17. evaluate
18. interview
19. recall
20. question

UNIT 4

Answer Key

Thinking of You

Wrap It Up, Anthology, p. 115

1. The first greeting cards celebrated Valentine's Day and New Year's Day.

2. Paper cards and e-cards are alike because you can send them for almost any occasion; both kinds of cards can express emotion; and both help you stay in touch with people.

3. Sample response: Cards exist for almost every occasion and offer a valuable way for people to communicate with one another.

4. Sample response: To find an animated card that makes noise, you would need to look on the World Wide Web.

5. Sample response: The next big change in greeting cards might be e-cards that include video and sound clips that the sender records using a digital camera.

6. Sample response: I think a paper card is better because it lasts and it is something you can keep and save to remember someone's feelings. E-cards, on the other hand, usually disappear after you view them and are not something that you save and remember.

Connect to the Big Question

Sample response: I think greeting cards work well as a form of communication. Sometimes they help to express difficult emotions, like saying you are sorry, and they make it easy to communicate with people who are far away.

Vocabulary Exercise, Writing Journal, p. 107

What do you think is the best way to transmit a message from one person to another? Even if a friend lives across the ocean in Europe, you can send transatlantic communication! A happy message can transform your friend's mood. Using a computer is one way to transfer a greeting. If you can connect to a camera, that is even better. A smile is a greeting that no one needs to translate.

Word on the Wire

Wrap It Up, Anthology, p. 119

1. Three reasons to ban cell phones in school are: the ringing upsets lessons, students may use them to play games, and students might be texting instead of paying attention.

2. Text messaging can hurt students' ability to spell and write well.

3. Sample response: One positive use of cell phones is that they help families and friends communicate. One negative use of cell phones is students cheating on tests.

4. Sample response: One way to solve the problem of cell phone use in schools is to have schools teach students about appropriate educational uses of cell phones.

5. Sample response: People say they are unable to get along without their cell phones because they have become very dependent on them, they need them for safety, and they feel good using them to stay in touch with others.

6. Sample response: Cell phones and text messaging can have good uses in the classroom if they are used to communicate assignments with teachers and do research related to assignments.

Connect to the Big Question

Sample response: I think students should be allowed to have cell phones in the classroom, but that they should be turned off while the teacher is teaching, during tests, and any time students are supposed to be doing class work.

Vocabulary Exercise, Writing Journal, p. 111

Long ago, it would have been hard to predict how cell phones would change people's lives. I try not to prejudge people who speak loudly on the phone at the movie theater, but those people can ruin the previews! My parents prepay my bill so that I have a limited number of minutes. Having a cell phone is a great precaution in case of an emergency.

A Show of Strength

Wrap It Up, Anthology, p. 123

1. The three heroes are Jeremy Hernandez, 20; Wesley Autrey, 50; and Alize Spry, 12.

2. Jeremy Hernandez helped rescue students from a bus on a collapsed bridge in Minneapolis, Minnesota. Wesley Autrey jumped onto subway tracks to save a man who had collapsed, pulling him to the center as a subway train passed above them. Alize Spry saved her four brothers and sisters when a fire started in their home by calling 911 and getting the children to a safer place in the house until help could arrive.

3. Planning for an emergency is important, but people who are heroes respond to unexpected disasters quickly, often putting their own lives at risk.

4. Sample response: These heroes reacted quickly and put their own lives at risk in order to save others. They all believed that what they were doing was the right thing.

5. Sample response: Jeremy Hernandez talks about how fear helped him act fast to save others as well as himself.

6. Sample response: I think Wesley Autrey is the most heroic. The other two people were already in dangerous situations when they acted heroically. However, when Wesley jumped onto the tracks, he left safety and put himself in danger in order to help a stranger.

Connect to the Big Question
Sample response: I think real-life heroes show courage by thinking about the safety and survival of others rather than putting their own safety first.

Vocabulary Exercise, Writing Journal, p. 115

The newscaster asked the witness to (call, (recall)) what happened during the tornado. The witness ((stated,) restated) what she saw. A man walking by a building heard a loud crash. He quickly ((reacted,) action) when he saw a woman pinned under a fallen roof. When he (viewed, (reviewed)) his actions later, the man said he saw someone in danger, so he just did what he could do to help.

The Big Money

Wrap It Up, Anthology, p. 127

1. The president of the United States made the least, $400,000.

2. CEOs, big entertainers, and star athletes are alike because all are paid a lot and usually are the best at what they do. They are different because of the kind of work they do, such as perform, entertain, and lead a company, and the kind of education and training required to do work.

3. Sample response: A teacher and CEO are alike because both have important jobs and may work long hours and have special training. They are different because one manages a company, while the other manages a classroom. Teachers are also paid much less than CEOs.

4. Sample response: Everyday people help create stars because they pay to see the stars perform and buy things that the stars advertise. We also buy magazines and watch TV shows about stars, which helps people become bigger stars.

5. Sample response: I can conclude that we pay a lot of attention to stars and want to know a lot of details about their private lives.

6. Sample response: If I disagree about how much money a star makes, I can stop seeing them perform or entertain. I can also stop buying products that the star creates or advertises.

Connect to the Big Question

Sample response: I think the message we send by the salaries we pay to stars is that they are more valuable than average people and they are the best at what they do.

Pay Days

Wrap It Up, Anthology, p. 131

1. The article discusses the difficult aspect of how teens can get money to spend as they want.

2. The main reason families give allowances is to teach kids to manage money, to pay them for doing chores, to give them money to do with as they please.

3. Some families think teens should be paid for doing chores, but others think that kids should be expected to do chores as part of their family responsibilities.

4. Sample response: If teens did not receive allowances, there might be a lot less spending on teen products, teens might not learn how to manage money, and many might want to get part-time jobs to provide spending money.

5. Sample response: The article shows that teens earn an average of $30 per week, but that this money comes from different sources, such as chores, allowance, and gifts.

6. Sample response: I think teens who have to work for their money probably spend less because they know how hard it is to earn the money. If your parents give you money every time you ask, you probably spend a lot more.

Connect to the Big Question

Sample response: When families pay teens allowances, I think it gives the message that they want teens to learn about how to handle money and how to make choices on how to spend it.

The Music Mix

Wrap It Up, Anthology, p. 135

1. The article compares music to a salad.
2. The three main ingredients of music are rhythm, melody, and harmony.
3. Recordings made it easier to share sounds with different regions and other musicians.
4. Sample response: You can conclude that people have used music to protest things they object to and as a way of expressing political and social beliefs.
5. Sample response: I think people will continue to create new types of music, and music in the United States will be influenced by music from other countries.
6. Sample response: I like all types of music because different types of music create different moods and feelings and tell something about the culture or era from which the music came.

Connect to the Big Question

Sample response: I think when music takes a different form, it does send a different message. It reflects how times have changed. Kids want to have their own sounds and their own forms of expression that are different from those of their parents.

Vocabulary Exercise, Writing Journal, p. 127

What is the <u>prescription</u> for a better mood? Sometimes it is music! <u>Scribble</u> the titles of a few of your favorite songs. Close your eyes and imagine you are listening to them. What feelings can you <u>describe</u>? Do you feel better yet?

Follow Your Star

Wrap It Up, Anthology, p. 139

1. People want to follow a leader as a natural way of protecting themselves.
2. Heroes of the past were known for doing great acts rather than for their images like today's celebrities. Past heroes were also self-made, while today's celebrities are usually created by the media.
3. "Celebrity worship syndrome" is when people are so interested in a celebrity that the celebrity becomes important to their lives and people think of the celebrity as a friend.
4. Sample response: The media help create celebrities, and by constantly telling us what celebrities are doing, the media increase celebrities' popularity.
5. Sample response: To change the influence celebrities have on me, I could choose to follow only those who set a positive example. I could also choose not to buy things just because a celebrity advertises them.
6. Sample response: I think most of the celebrities in advertisements are positive role models because companies do not want to use people who break the law or are in trouble to talk about their products.

Connect to the Big Question

Sample response: I think people's fascination with celebrities is a way of forgetting about their own troubles and dreaming about what life would be like to be rich and famous. Sometimes people also feel better when they realize that celebrities are just human and make mistakes and have problems just like everyone else.

Vocabulary Exercise, Writing Journal, p. 131

1. graphology
2. geology
3. cardiology
4. morphology

The Age Factor

Wrap It Up, Anthology, p. 143

1. Jim Morris made a deal with his team that if they won their district championship, he would try out for the Major Leagues.

2. Older pro athletes should be valued because they are wise, well-rounded, and can make good decisions.

3. "Your body is your office" means that your body is what you use to do your job, so you need to take good care of it.

4. Sample response: You can conclude from McManus, Morris, and Favre that older athletes have as much talent and commitment as younger athletes, and they have a passion for the game.

5. Sample response: I know someone who decided to learn to ski at 55. Many people tried to tell her she was too old to start at that age even though she was in good shape. Once she learned, she became just as good as others who had been skiing for years.

6. Sample response: The older athlete probably has physical limitations that he or she did not have while younger, such as less speed, slower reactions, and less flexibility. However, the older athlete has more experience that he or she can apply, more practice, and a better ability to anticipate what might happen.

Connect to the Big Question

Sample response: The message about aging that athletes communicate is that your age is less important than your passion and commitment. If your body is able to perform at a high level, you are just as important a competitor as younger players.

Word Bank Quiz

1. communicate
2. speak
3. listen
4. entertain
5. media
6. express
7. enrich
8. technology
9. transmit
10. inform
11. produce
12. describe
13. source
14. reveal
15. learn
16. react
17. method
18. argue
19. teach
20. contribute

Answer Key

How Attitude Helps

Real-Life Connection, p. 148

1. False
2. True
3. False
4. True

Wrap It Up, Anthology, p. 151

1. Peale wrote *The Power of Positive Thinking*
2. People with a positive personality look for the good in situations. Those with a negative personality focus on the bad.
3. The woman on the talk show made a list of things in her life that she could imagine being good. She gave up worrying and seized the power to take positive steps. As a result, she started her own business, got married, and had a family.
4. Sample response: Some people who have positive goals fail because of circumstances outside their control. Every person cannot expect success every time, but a positive attitude can help a person accept failure and continue to try.
5. Sample response: Setting positive goals might have negative effects if a person feels overwhelmed by his or her goals. Sometimes people expect change to happen quickly, and when it does not they feel let down.
6. Sample response: Some changes that would make my life more positive are to finish my homework for every class every day and make sure I remember to bring it to school. Another positive change would be to stop arguing with my older sister.

Connect to the Big Question

Sample response: I do not think that negative thoughts are keeping me down because I try to look on the bright side of life. I know that some people look at the glass as half-empty and some people see it as half-full, and I always try to see the good in a situation.

Happiness: A Two-Way Street?

Wrap It Up, Anthology, p. 155

1. RAK stands for Random Acts of Kindness Foundation.
2. Oprah Winfrey's Angel Network raised $9 million for one program in South Africa and $15 million for victims of hurricanes Katrina and Rita.
3. People get involved in giving because they want to make a difference for others. Charity work gives people a feeling of pride and purpose.
4. Sample response: The Angel Network appeals to so many people because Oprah asked people to collect spare change. People felt that it was easy to make a small donation, and all the spare change added up to big dollars.
5. Sample response: The advice I would give to a company that wanted to encourage its employees to give would be to organize a charity event because the employees will feel proud of the company as a result. Working together to raise money for a charity could also bring the employees closer together because they shared a goal and succeeded in helping others.
6. Sample response: In order to find more happiness than I now have, I could make a few changes. I could consider how I might help people who are less fortunate. By getting involved in giving to others, or collecting spare change for an organization like the Angel Network, I would be making a contribution to someone who needed it, and that would give me a good feeling.

Connect to the Big Question

Sample response: I think a person needs to think of others and try not to be selfish in order to be happy. People help others because it is unselfish, and because they get a good feeling from giving. Helping others also gives people a purpose in life and a feeling of satisfaction.

Called Out

Wrap It Up, Anthology, p. 159

1. Intervention is an attempt to help people escape from harmful habits or threats.
2. Three warning signs that someone needs help are: depression, erratic behavior like changing plans suddenly, or falling grades.
3. A teen may need help if he or she is on drugs or alcohol, has lost so much weight he or she no longer looks healthy, or spends too much time alone on the Internet.

4. Sample response: Some teens develop problems that might need intervention because they are under pressure and turn to self-destructive behaviors. Not every teen is prone to self-destructive behaviors, however.

5. Sample response: Some interventions might cause more problems than they solve because they are not handled properly. It takes a trained professional, like a doctor, to organize an intervention.

6. Sample response: I think one thing that could help prevent at-risk kids from developing serious problems is a classroom meeting. In a classroom meeting, kids can discuss problems they are having in school and ways to solve those problems. When kids know they can trust their teacher, they may also be able to share problems they are having outside of school.

Connect to the Big Question

Sample response: If someone told me they had a friend with a serious problem, I would ask them what the problem was. Then I would recommend that they ask an adult whether or not they should intervene. Sometimes kids want to help a friend, but they do not know what to do. When you are worried about a friend, it is important to get a trusted adult to help you.

Vocabulary Exercise, Writing Journal, p. 149

We have a clear (differ, (difference,) different) of opinion about this. I think the actor's (perform, performing, (performance)) was great. I know his voice was (annoyance, (annoying)), and I usually don't like movies with so much ((violence,) violent). But I still think his acting was truly brilliant.

Pushing Buttons

Real-Life Connection, p. 160
1. False
2. False
3. False
4. False

Wrap It Up, Anthology, p. 163
1. Bullies spread rumors on the Internet through e-mails, instant messages, or chat-room taunts.
2. One third of students bullied are not bothered, some are bothered by the bullying, and one third are angry. Many victims respond with mixed emotions.

3. Bullying can affect the way a student acts at home, at school, and with friends. Bullying may even affect how a kid acts online.

4. Sample response: I think cyberbullies continue their online behavior because it is hard to get caught. Bullies can hide their identity online.

5. Sample response: A victim of bullying may become a bully because he or she is angry about getting picked on. Some kids turn to bullying for revenge.

6. Sample response: Gossip crosses a line and becomes harmful when people's feelings get hurt or lies are spread on the Internet.

Connect to the Big Question

Sample response: I think the best way to handle gossip and bullying is to follow the advice in the article: stop, block, and tell. Stop communicating with a bully, block the bully online so he cannot send you e-mails or IMs, and tell someone that you have been bullied so the bully will stop picking on you and other people.

Vocabulary Exercise, Writing Journal, p. 153
1. a
2. b

Word Bank Quiz
1. consider
2. reveal
3. characteristics
4. appreciate
5. assumption
6. perspectives
7. image
8. appearance
9. perception
10. ignore
11. complete
12. appearance
13. bias
14. reflect
15. setting
16. reaction
17. define
18. identify
19. perspectives
20. focus

Answer Key

The Great Dress Debate

Wrap It Up, Anthology, p. 171

1. Clothes that might be linked with gangs, such as bandannas, hoods, neck chains, and sunglasses, as well as clothes that might encourage drug or alcohol use or racism have been banned in schools.
2. Some people support dress codes because they think dress codes decrease crime, encourage attendance, and increase school pride.
3. Some people are against dress codes because they feel there is no proof that dress codes improve schools, and they believe students should have a right to express themselves and show their differences.
4. Sample response: Certain kinds of clothes might cause violence by displaying gang symbols. This could encourage rival gang members to fight in school.
5. Sample response: I would not allow students to wear jeans, flip-flops, or sweatshirts and sweatpants.
6. Sample response: I believe that a strict dress code is better because even though it is a dress code, students can still have the opportunity to express themselves within certain parameters. A dress code would not allow expression.

Connect to the Big Question

Sample response: I think following a dress code is more important than individual expression. People can express themselves as individuals all they want outside of school. Without a dress code, students might wear things or do things that limit others' ability to learn or be themselves.

Vocabulary Exercise, Writing Journal, p. 159

1. amazement
2. merriment
3. settle
4. Sample response: It is wrong to make judgments about others.

Commanding the Weather

Real-Life Connection, Anthology, p. 172

1. False
2. True
3. False
4. True

Wrap It Up, Anthology, p. 175

1. Clouds are seeded by scattering chemicals from planes or shooting them into clouds.
2. Weather modifications could be helpful because they could provide water for people, supply rain for crops, and lessen the effects of severe storms like hurricanes or tornadoes.
3. The arguments against weather modification include a lack of proof that techniques like cloud seeding work; a concern about the use of toxic chemicals; and a debate about whose interests should be served by changing the weather.
4. Sample response: An international treaty might ban weather modification for hostile purposes because most countries probably consider this an inappropriate way of fighting and one that harms innocent civilians as well as troops.
5. Sample response: If weather modification were used, there might be more food and water supplies throughout the world; there might be less damage and loss of life from severe weather; and there might be warfare as countries battle over who had the right to control the weather.
6. Sample response: If I controlled the weather, I would make sure that dry parts of the world had enough rainfall for people to grow crops and supply their basic food and water needs. I would prioritize these uses over recreational ones, like having dry weather for the Olympics or nice weather for coastal tourists.

Connect to the Big Question

Sample response: I think we should control the weather only if we can reach agreement about how it can be safely used for the greatest human benefit.

Vocabulary Exercise, Writing Journal, p. 163

1. V
2. V
3. N

Restoring Cities from the Ground Up

Wrap It Up, Anthology, p. 179

1. Two goals of the Luv Ur Block project are to unify teens and to clean up neighborhood litter.
2. One result of Albany's Make a Difference Day is that people take pride in the places where they live.

3. Working in an urban garden can benefit young people because it provides jobs, education in farming, and affordable healthful food for the community.

4. Sample response: Some people might be opposed to urban gardens because they would rather see a business that generates tax revenue occupy the space.

5. Sample response: I could use this article's information to make a proposal to people in my community to start similar projects.

6. Sample response: All the projects mentioned in the article benefit the people who live in the community. They also improve the neighborhoods by cleaning up trash.

Connect to the Big Question

Sample response: I think urban gardens can help turn around the community, because the article gives a number of examples of successful efforts. I think these gardens help people feel pride in their neighborhoods and help neighbors get to know one another.

Vocabulary Exercise, Writing Journal, p. 167

1. courage
2. fame
3. joy
4. poison

What It Takes to Lead

Wrap It Up, Anthology, p. 183

1. A selfless leader is a leader willing to make personal sacrifices and not think only of him- or herself.

2. Jonas is selfless because he puts his own life at risk in order to save others. Krzyzewski, on the other hand, is selfless because he does not take all the credit for the accomplishments of his basketball teams. Both are selfless because they put others' interests ahead of their own.

3. Ling shows leadership by putting herself at risk in order to inform and educate others about the world's injustices.

4. Sample response: Selfless leaders can inspire teams to work better together rather than as individuals trying to be great and get credit for their accomplishments.

5. Sample response: My friends mother is selfless because she risked her life to save a child that was caught in a river.

6. Sample response: Learning from leaders around me might prepare me to be a leader someday.

Connect to the Big Question

Sample response: A good leader has qualities like selflessness and a commitment to helping people and improving people's lives.

Vocabulary Exercise, Writing Journal, p. 171

Row one: a pair of animals pulling together

Row two: belief or story passed down over time that may or may not be true

Rebuilding Communities

Wrap It Up, Anthology, p. 187

1. The tornado caused destruction of homes, schools, churches, businesses, and roads as well as loss of power, water, and jobs for residents of Greensburg.

2. New Orleans citizens in Austin kept their culture alive by holding a cultural event that included jazz and Creole food.

3. Qualities that bring communities together in time of hardship include focusing on the big picture and not individual losses; helping neighbors in need; having a willingness to listen to, comfort, and share faith with one another; and showing community pride.

4. Sample response: Creating a new kind of town for Greensburg could help people focus on the future rather than the past and build a better community than what existed before.

5. Sample response: I would help the community recover by volunteering to help clean up after the disaster. I would also help distribute food and water to those who needed it.

6. Sample response: In all of the disasters, people had to leave their homes or completely lost their homes.

Connect to the Big Question

Sample response: To help a community unite and rebuild, people have to have pride in their town and have a positive outlook for the future. Often they have to be patient and willing to help and be helped by others.

Vocabulary Exercise, Writing Journal, p. 175

1. beautify
2. speech
3. horrify
4. electrify

The Irresistible Urban Myth

Wrap It Up, Anthology, p. 191

1. Urban myths take the form of funny stories, shocking stories, sympathy scams, and cautionary tales.

2. A cautionary tale is one that warns people about possible danger.

3. People share urban myths to practice their storytelling, to get a thrill by playing a prank on people, and to make people feel selfless and giving.

4. Sample response: People might repeat stories without checking their truth because they enjoy telling stories and adding their own twist to a story.

5. Sample response: I have not heard any urban myths but when I do, I might pass them along to practice my storytelling.

6. Sample response: Gossiping is worse because it is directed toward real people and often hurts their feelings.

Connect to the Big Question

Sample response: Urban myths can help an individual feel connected to his or her community. They can be a form of entertainment, and although they aren't true, they can warn people to be careful.

Vocabulary Exercise, Writing Journal, p. 179

1. union
2. unify
3. unison

The Ripple Effect

Wrap It Up, Anthology, p. 195

1. Teens for Humanity is dedicated to bringing students together to share experiences, creating a supportive environment, diffusing violence, finding assistance, and holding special events.

2. Jennifer Staple created Unit for Sight after she worked in an eye doctor's office and saw how many people lost their sight because of preventable diseases.

3. When one person does something positive to help others, the person's actions ripple to other people, creating a larger force for change.

4. Sample response: So many schools have started TFH chapters because there is a real need for the support and services this organization offers.

5. Sample response: You can learn from Jennifer Staple that just one young person can make a huge difference. Even though Staple did not have special training, she began a program that now helps millions of people worldwide.

6. Sample response: These programs are similar in that they were started by individuals who wanted to address problems they saw in the world. Both programs have spread beyond the place where they started and help many people.

Connect to the Big Question

Sample response: I think small individual efforts can make a huge difference in the world. When the individual starts something positive, more people join forces, but without the one individual in the beginning, nothing might happen.

Vocabulary Exercise, Writing Journal, p. 183

1. division
2. dividends
3. divisive

Trickster Appeal Revealed!

Wrap It Up, Anthology, p. 199

1. The trickster tradition comes from myths and folklore.

2. A trickster character can be mean and funny at the same time; can cause his or her own problems; may disobey the rules; and can get out of tricky situations.

3. Some people think Bugs Bunny and Captain Jack Sparrow are lovable characters because Bugs Bunny outsmarts his enemy in funny ways, while Captain Jack Sparrow says and does what he wants, often getting into trouble but getting out of it with style.

4. People admire tricksters because they make us laugh and they appeal to the rebel in us. They entertain us with their creativity and cleverness.

5. Sample response: Trickster characters can inspire people to find clever solutions; tricksters can also keep society from becoming too restricted.

6. Sample response: A trickster's antics might cross the line by showing bad behavior and being disrespectful of adults, rules, and authority.

Connect to the Big Question

Sample response: I think trickster characters are appealing because they are funny and people can often identify with them because they are underdogs. They are also usually clever and creative at getting out of tricky situations.

Word Bank Quiz

1. community
2. tradition
3. environment
4. duty
5. unify
6. individual
7. family
8. voice
9. persuade
10. group
11. various
12. team
13. diversity
14. common
15. unique
16. custom
17. argue
18. completely
19. culture
20. ethnicity

USING THE GRAMMAR, USAGE, AND MECHANICS HANDBOOK IN THE WRITING JOURNAL

The Grammar, Usage, and Mechanics Handbook combines explanations with practice exercises. Therefore, it can be used for review as well as reference. More specifically, you might use the Handbook to do the following activities.

Peer Evaluations In the Check It and Fix It section for each writing assignment, students are directed to use the Handbook to look up principles of grammar, mechanics, and usage. Model how to use the Handbook table of contents. On the chalkboard, write in lowercase letters the name of a landmark building (for example, *empire state building*), and ask students to look up how to capitalize the name. Direct students to scan the table of contents on page 189 of their Writing Journal to find the section titled Capitalization. Together, turn to page 219 and find the capitalization rule that applies (No. 2: Capitalize the proper name of a place). Use the rule to capitalize the name correctly.

Individual, Partner, or Group Review As you evaluate student writing, list the kinds of errors each student makes. Use the list to help the student make a personalized proofreading list so that he or she knows the areas on which to focus. Help students set priorities. If a student has several areas of difficulty, select two or three important principles to work on. Follow up by assigning pertinent review exercises. You might ask students to complete exercises individually as homework or to do exercises in class with a partner or in a small group. If you wish, make answer keys available to students so that they can evaluate their own answers. Then review the principles that give difficulty.

Mini Lessons As an alternative, use the Handbook to do mini grammar lessons a few days each week. Pose a frequently asked grammar question to the class, and use the Handbook to answer it. The following Student FAQs may used to plan mini lessons.

NOUNS		
When do I need to add an *-s* to a noun?	Regular Plurals	190
Which is right: *citys* or *cities? Lifes* or *lives?*	Special Noun Plurals	191
Should I say *two women* or *two womens?*	Irregular Plurals	192
What is the difference between *'s* and *s'?*	Possessive Nouns	192
PRONOUNS		
Should I say *I* or *me? My* or *mine?*	Subject and Object Pronouns	193
	Pronouns in Compounds	194
	Possessive Pronouns	194
Which is right: *this, that,* or *them? These* or *those?*	Demonstrative Pronouns	195
Should I use *their* or *his* or *her?*	Indefinite Pronouns	195
	Pronoun-Antecedent Agreement	196

VERBS

ADJECTIVES AND ADVERBS

SENTENCE STRUCTURE

MECHANICS

Answer Key

Regular Plurals, p. 190

1. ways
3. Dolphins
4. partners
5. classmates
6. homes

Special Noun Plurals, p. 191

1. lives
2. communities
3. boxes
4. roofs
5. autos
6. heroes

Irregular Plurals, p. 192

1. people
2. women
3. tooth
4. men

Possessive Nouns, p. 192

1. sister's
2. guests'
3. Mary's

Subject and Object Pronouns, p. 193

1. They
2. them
3. He
4. they

Pronouns in Compounds, p. 194

1. Ashlyn and I
2. She and I
3. her and me
4. she and I
5. Ashlyn and me

Possessive Pronouns, p. 194

1. mine
2. yours
3. their
4. Her

Demonstrative Pronouns, p. 195

1. That
2. this
3. those

Indefinite Pronouns, p. 195

1. Everyone *S*
2. Most *P*
3. Many *P*
4. Anybody *S*
5. Several *P*

Pronoun-Antecedent Agreement, p. 196

1. his or her
2. his or her
3. his or her
4. his or her

Relative Pronouns, p. 197

Sample responses:

1. My poem was the shortest that was in the contest.
2. Judges who read my poem liked it.
3. I was one of only a few students who wrote a nature poem.
4. I am happy that I won.

Action and Linking Verbs, p. 198

1. is
2. jumps
3. slides
4. are
5. claps
6. bow
7. enjoyed
8. was

Present Tense Verbs, p. 199

1. takes
2. draws
3. admire
4. wants
5. say
6. submit

Tricky Present Tense Verbs, p. 200

2. isn't OR is not
3. doesn't OR does not
4. have
6. does
7. isn't OR is not
8. has

Agreement with Compound Subjects, p. 201

2. are
3. has
4. knows

Agreement in Questions, p. 201

1. Are
2. do
3. have
4. does
5. Is

Past and Perfect Tenses, p. 202

1. has wanted
2. had saved
3. realized
4. informed
5. haven't

Irregular Verbs 1: Past and Perfect of *To Be*, p. 203

1. was
2. were
3. were
4. was
5. have

Irregular Verbs 3: Past and Perfect That Change Vowels, p. 204

1. spoke
2. seen
3. broken
4. rang
5. knew
6. forgotten

Irregular Verbs 4: Past and Perfect That Change Completely, p. 205

1. bought
2. gone
3. flew
4. brought
5. thought
6. found
7. sold
8. did

Verbs as Describers, p. 206

2. fried
3. mashed
4. frozen

Future Tense, p. 206

1. will go
2. will visit
3. will eat
4. will return

Progressive Tenses, p. 207

Sample responses:
1. I was writing.
2. I will be visiting my cousin.
3. I am studying.

Modals, p. 207

1. should participate
2. would join
3. might play
4. would have played

Articles, p. 208

2. a union
3. a drawing, photograph, or painting
6. the rain water

Adjectives That Compare, p. 209

1. older
2. youngest
3. most famous
4. more popular
5. cheaper

Irregular Adjectives, p. 210

1. better
2. more
3. most
4. worst

Double Comparisons, p. 210

2. longer
3. warmer
4. happiest

The *-ly* Adverb Ending, p. 211

1. loudly
2. constantly
3. happily
4. quickly
5. enthusiastically

Good and *Well,* p. 212

1. well
2. well
3. good

Double Negatives, p. 212

1. any sleep OR hardly any
2. wasn't ever OR was never
3. didn't want to do anything

Prepositional Phrases, p. 213

1. in my school
2. of equipment
3. After school
4. from my friends
5. to those messages

Coordinating Conjunctions, p. 214

1. and
2. but
3. so
4. or
5. yet
6. and
7. but
8. for

Subordinating Conjunctions, p. 215

1. When I grow up
2. because I like helping people
3. Though nursing is hard work

GRAMMAR HANDBOOK Answer Key

Correlative Conjunctions, p. 215

1. Both . . . and
2. not only . . . but also
3. Neither . . . nor

Clauses, p. 216

1. when I gave mine
2. because she loves horses
3. As she talked
4. after Laura spoke
5. Though I tried to be calm
6. than I am
7. Before I knew it
8. than I expected

Run-on Sentences, p. 217

Sample responses:

1. Pizza is a very old kind of food. It has probably been around since the Stone Age.
3. Tomatoes were not brought to Europe until the 1500s, so the first Italian pizzas did not have tomato sauce.
4. Today, pizza is one of the most popular foods in the world. Millions of people eat it.

Fragments, p. 218

Sample responses:

1. I
2. go
3. I go to neighborhood restaurants the most often
4. is
5. there is probably a restaurant for you.

Capitalization, p. 219

1. Aunt Cicily
2. York
3. Statue of Liberty
4. Then
5. *A Raisin in the Sun*
6. Italian

End Marks, p. 220

1. question mark
2. period
3. period OR exclamation point
4. period
5. exclamation point OR period

Commas, p. 221

1. contest, Frank
2. Really,
3. routines, and
4. June 10, 2008,
5. Russ, my best friend,
6. Russ, Allan, and I
7. Detroit, Michigan,
8. cheers,
9. In fact,

Apostrophes, p. 222

1. Steve's
2. It's
3. He's
4. yours

Quotation Marks, p. 222

1. "Did you do your homework?"
2. "Two Kinds"
3. "I started to read it," Bob said, "but I fell asleep."

Spelling, p. 223

1. receive
2. supplies
3. neighbor
4. sloppily
5. amazed
6. dazzling
7. players
8. guys
9. craziest
10. winners

GRAPHIC ORGANIZERS

Organizers guide vocabulary development, support comprehension strategies, bolster students' preparation for reading, or assess students' learning of key concepts related to the Big Questions.

Cause and Effect Map

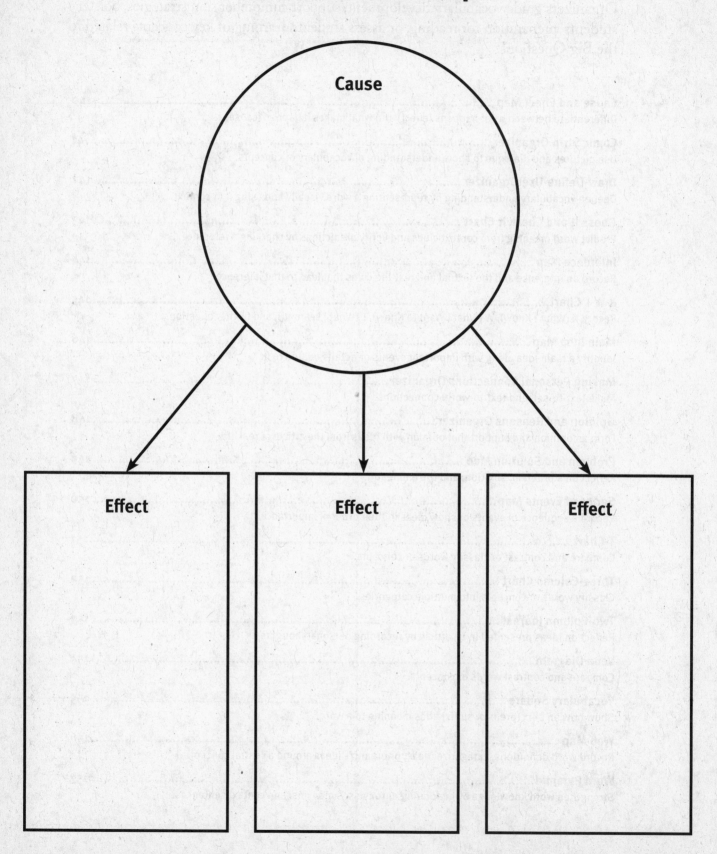

Comic Strip Organizer

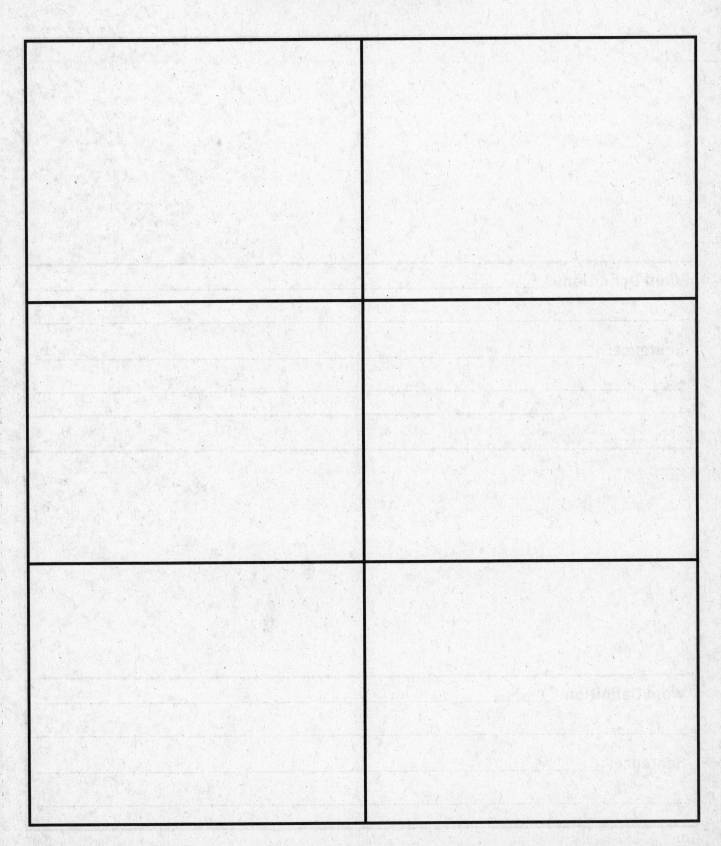

Draw-Define-Use Organizer

Word Definition: _____

_____

Sentence: _____

_____

Word Definition: _____

_____

Sentence: _____

_____

Guess It and Check It Chart

Word	Context Clues	Guess	Check

Inference Map

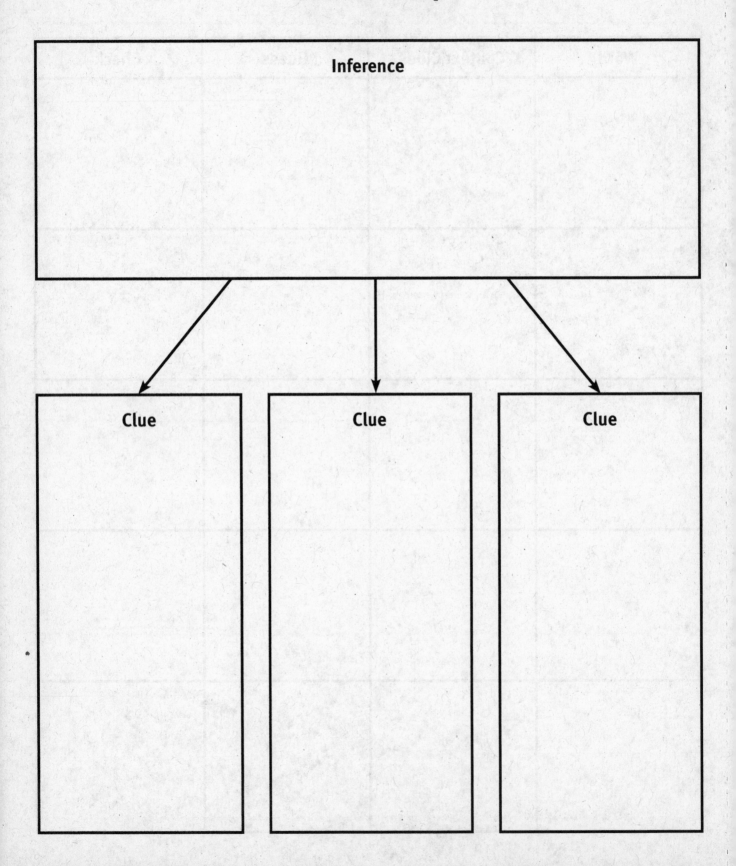

Inference

Clue

Clue

Clue

K-W-L Chart

K: What I Know	W: What I Want to Know	L: What I Learned	Questions After Reading

Main Idea Map

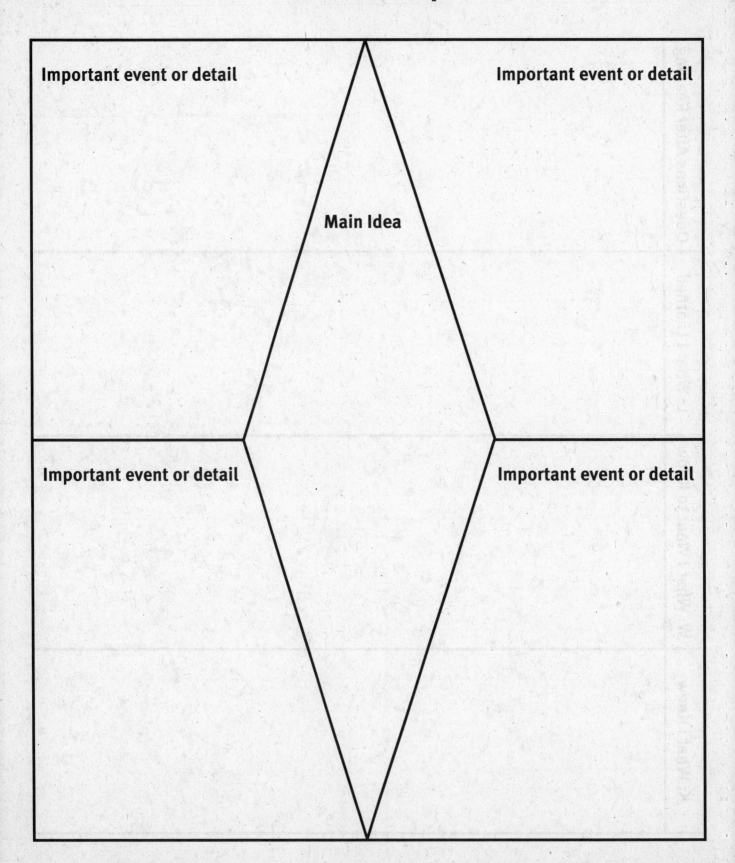

Important event or detail

Important event or detail

Main Idea

Important event or detail

Important event or detail

Making Personal Connections Organizer

What is being explained or described in the text:

Connection to My Personal Experiences	Connection to Other Things (movies, books, other people)
1.	1.
2.	2.
3.	3.

Opinion and Reasons Organizer

Opinion

Reasons

Problem and Solution Map

Problem

Solution	Response

End Result

Series of Events Map

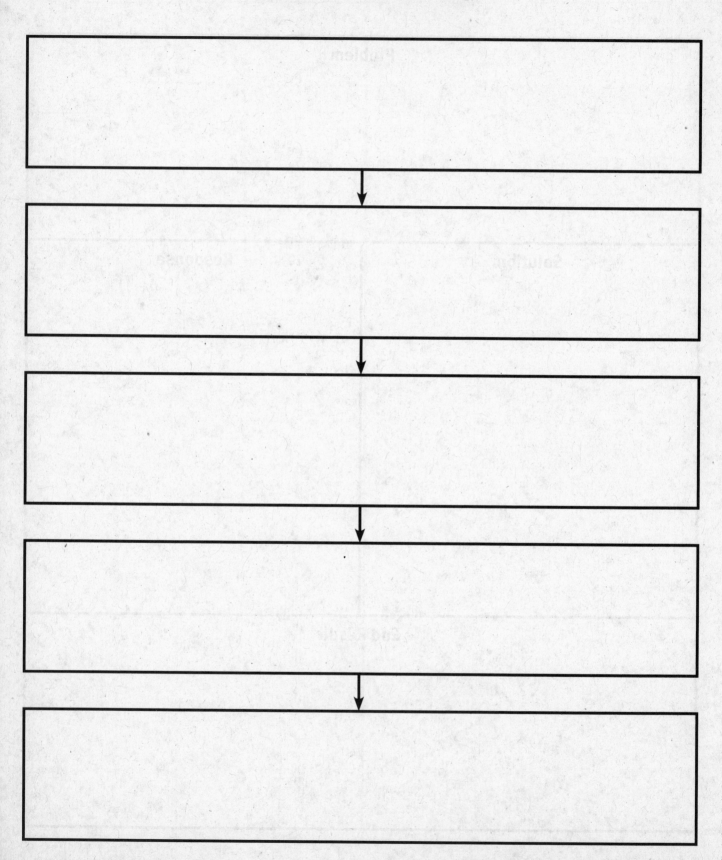

T-Chart

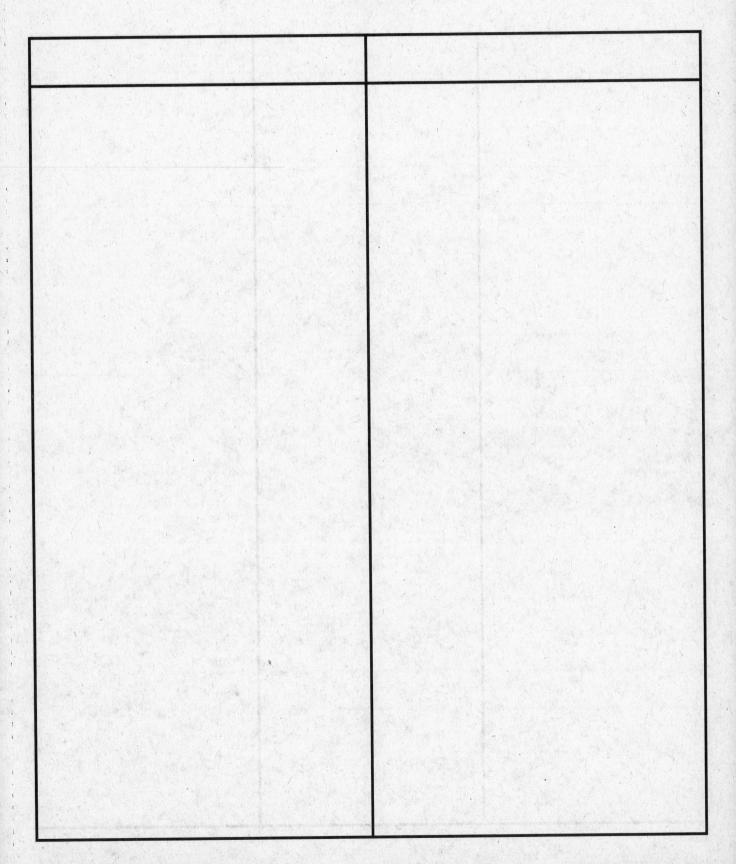

Three-Column Chart

Two-Column Journal

Ideas from the Article	My Thoughts

Venn Diagram

Vocabulary Square

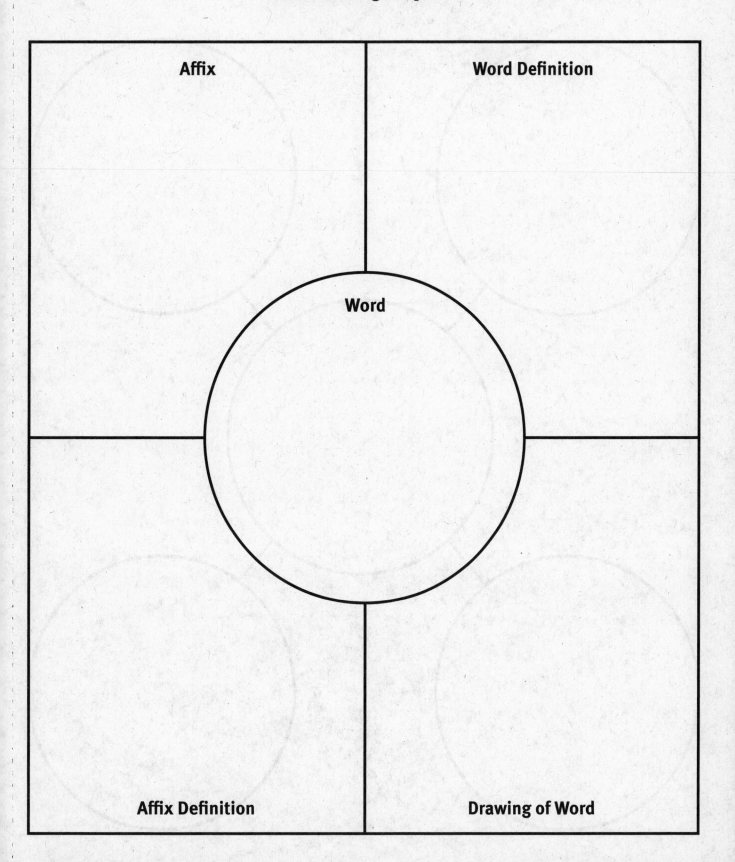

Affix

Word Definition

Word

Affix Definition

Drawing of Word

Web Map

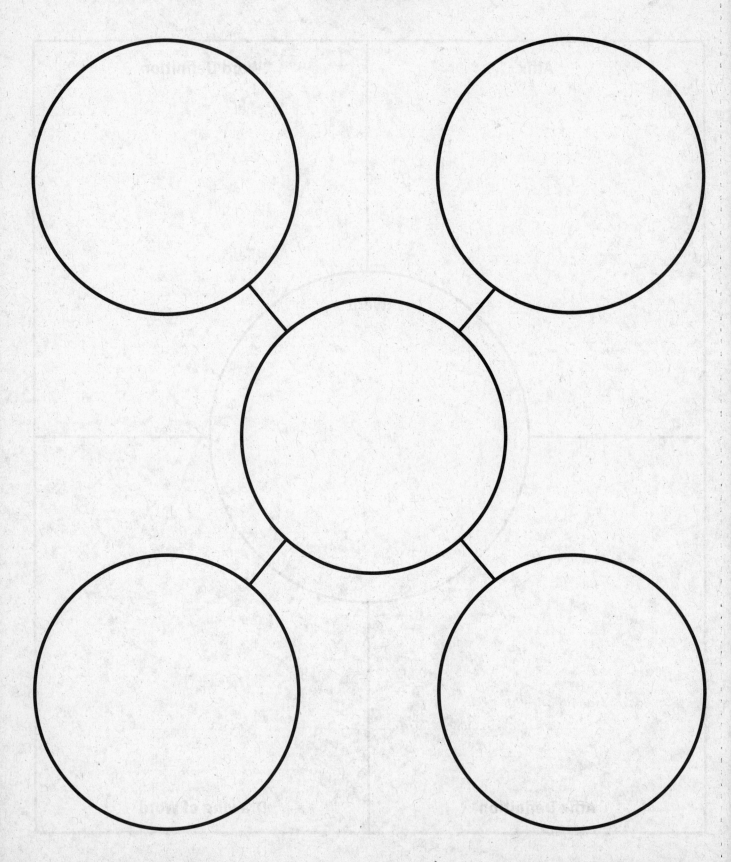

Word Pyramid

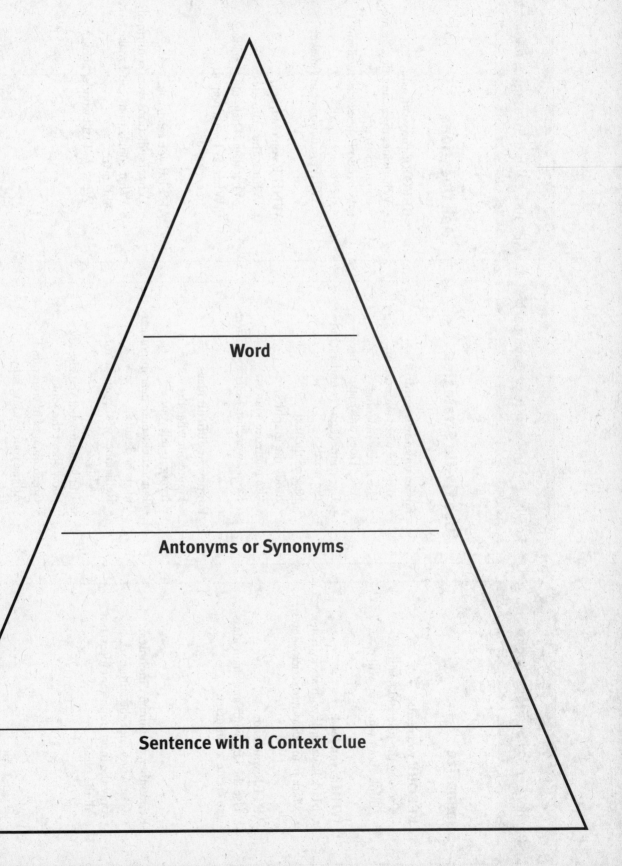

Word

Antonyms or Synonyms

Sentence with a Context Clue

Reality Central **Strategy Bookmarks**

Reality Central **Strategy Bookmark**

Summarize

BEFORE you read:
- Preview the title and headings.
- Think about what you will read.

WHILE you read:
- Mark key words with sticky notes.
- Mark main ideas with sticky notes.

AFTER you read:
- Use the key words and main ideas to create a summary.

Remember, a summary includes:
- your words, not the author's.
- only the most important ideas, not all the ideas.

Reality Central **Strategy Bookmark**

Use Fix-Up Strategies

For an unknown word:
- Skip the word and read on.
- Use a new meaning.
  Ask, "Does this make sense?"
- Use connections to understand the words.
- Reread the text.
- Study the graphics.
- Use reference sources.
- Keep a word list. Refer to it often.

For new or difficult ideas:
- Figure out what the author is trying to tell you.
- Put a sticky note near important ideas or details.
- Remember your purpose for reading.
- Think about what you already know about the topic.
- Create images in your mind.
- Adjust your reading rate.

Reality Central **Strategy Bookmark**

Ask Questions

BEFORE you read, ask:
- What clues does the title give me about the text?
- What do I already know about this topic?
- What predictions can I make?

WHILE you read, ask:
- What is the main idea?
- What details help me visualize?
- What do I need help to understand?

AFTER you read, ask:
- What predictions were confirmed?
- What connections can I make to this text?
- What do I still wonder about?

Reality Central **Strategy Bookmarks**

Make Connections

Connect to Your Own Experiences

- What does the text remind you of from your own experiences?
- How are these situations alike?
- How does the connection help you understand the text?

Connect to the World

- How does the text remind you of something you have seen or heard about?
- How are these situations alike?
- How does the connection help you understand the text?

Connect to Other Texts

- What other text (print or media) does this article remind you of?
- How are the texts alike?
- How does the connection help you understand the text?

Preview, Predict, and Set Purposes

Preview Before you read, look at:

- the introduction
- the title
- photographs
- captions
- heads and subheads
- boldface words
- graphs, charts, and other visuals
- the questions at the end

Predict Answer these questions:

- Why did the author write this?
- What will I learn as I read it?
- What will the author tell me?

Set Purposes

- Am I reading for entertainment, to hear a message, or to find out information?
- Finish this sentence:
  As I read, I expect to find out _____

Make Inferences

Think about this equation as you read:

Background Knowledge
+ Clues from the Text = Inference!

List what you **know** about the topic:

_____
_____
_____

List **clues** from the text:

_____
_____
_____

What **inference** can you make?

_____
_____
_____

Reality Central **Strategy Bookmarks**

Reality Central **Strategy Bookmark**

Visualize

Use images to create a picture in your mind as you read.

What can you **see**?

What do you **hear**?

What can you **feel**?

What might you be able to **smell**?

Can you **taste** anything?

How do these images help you understand the text?

_____

_____

_____

_____

_____

Reality Central **Strategy Bookmark**

Read Fluently

Fluent reading is about reading rate, accuracy, and expression.

Reading Rate:

✓ Is this material difficult for you? Slow down!

✓ Is this material technical and full of facts? Slow down!

✓ Is the text easy for you to read? Speed up!

✓ Is this text a story rather than many facts? Speed up!

Accuracy:

If you are unsure of a word:

✓ "Try out" several words to see which one fits.

✓ Look for clues around the word.

✓ Reread or read on.

Expression:

✓ Look for commas. They tell you to pause.

✓ Look for periods. They tell you to take a longer pause.

✓ Look for question marks. They tell you to have a rise in your voice.

How do you read short sentences?

How do you read longer ones? Think about the emotion in your voice while you read.

Reality Central **Strategy Bookmark**

Determine Importance

Strategic readers can differentiate between what is important to know and what is interesting to know.

Important information is **relevant**. Information that is less important is **irrelevant**.

As you read, mark relevant information with sticky notes.

Use the relevant information to write a statement of main idea.

_____

_____

_____

_____

_____

_____

_____

Assessment Tools

Use the assessment tools at various points as you work with *Reality Central*. Assessments are designed to help inform your instruction. The results of assessments will help you plan how best to work with each student.

Retelling Rubric

Ask the student to retell you the important parts of a piece of expository text. Use this rubric to assess understanding of ideas, text structure, and key vocabulary.

Student Name: _____

Passage/Text: _____

Date: _____

4	• Accurately retells important concepts from the text in own words. • Organizes information using appropriate text structures throughout the retelling (such as sequential order, classification, cause and effect, compare and contrast, and so on). • Appropriately uses key vocabulary. • Synthesizes concepts from the text, using textual evidence and prior knowledge to draw inferences and generate original conclusions.
3	• Explains the main ideas and supporting details from the text in own words. • Organizes the information using appropriate text structure (such as sequential order, classification, cause and effect, compare and contrast, and so on). • Utilizes some key vocabulary. • Attempts to draw inferences/generalizations and supports them with textual evidence and prior knowledge.
2	• Demonstrates a partial understanding of the text, randomly restating facts/concepts, or relying heavily on the author's words. May copy some material from the text. • Organization is less defined; text structure is weak. • May utilize some key vocabulary. • May include inaccuracies or omissions.
1	• Relates a limited amount of information, conveying little or no understanding of the text. May copy extensively from the text. • May include some inaccuracies, omissions, or confusions. • May include information that is off-topic.

Phrasing and Fluency Checklist

Use this checklist to record oral reading behaviors.

Student Name: _____

Passage/Text: _____

Date: _____

When the student read orally, phrasing and fluency were:

_____ appropriate for the text, combining short and long phrases and considering punctuation

_____ in longer phrases

_____ in short phrases

_____ word by word

The student's reading rate was:

_____ adjusted properly to match text

_____ inconsistent

_____ too fast for the text

_____ too slow for the text

The number of correct words per minute _____

Recommended oral reading rates (Good, Kaminski, Barr, and Rasinski)

Grade	Oral Correct Words Per Minute
6	110–150
7	150–180
8+	180–200+

The student used the following strategies when encountering difficulty:

_____ rereading up to point of difficulty

_____ reading ahead

_____ using visual clues such as illustrations

_____ breaking words into syllables

_____ sounding out words letter by letter

_____ other. Describe:

_____

The student self-corrected when the miscues were the following:

_____ semantic (interfered with meaning)

_____ graphemic/phonemic (did not match the text)

_____ syntactic (did not sound like correct language)

Other observations that inform instruction:

_____

_____

_____

_____

Collaboration Rubric

Use this checklist to assess students' work in groups. Students can use this tool to assess their own participation in group activities.

Student Name: _____

Date: _____

CATEGORY	4	3	2	1
Focus and Participation	Stays focused on the task and what needs to be done. Self-directed and contributes to the group.	Focuses on the task and what needs to be done most of the time. Can be counted on by other group members.	Focuses on the task some of the time. Other group members need to remind the person to stay on task.	Lets others do the work. Rarely focuses on the task and what needs to be done.
Dependability	Follows through on tasks that are assigned and does not depend on others to do the work. Shares responsibility for tasks.	Follows through on most assigned tasks.	Does not follow through on most assigned tasks. Sometimes depends on others to do the work.	Depends on others to do the work. Does not follow through on assigned tasks.
Discussion Skills	Respectfully listens, interacts, discusses, and poses questions to all members of the team and helps to direct the group in reaching consensus.	Listens respectfully, interacts, discusses, and poses questions to others during discussions.	Has some difficulty respectfully listening and discussing.	Has great difficulty listening, may argue during discussions, and does not listen to others' opinions. May keep group from reaching consensus.
Solving Problems	Looks for and suggests solutions to problems.	When others suggest solutions, improves the solutions.	Does not suggest or improve solutions, but is willing to try out others' solutions.	Does not try to solve problems or help group members solve problems.
Teamwork	Has a positive attitude about working with the team in collaboration.	Usually has a positive attitude about the work of others on the team.	May be critical of the work of others.	Critical of the work of other group members.
Sharing Information	Gathers research if necessary and shares useful ideas with the group.	Provides some useful research and ideas to the group in discussion.	Sometimes provides useful research and ideas with the group.	Seldom provides useful ideas to the group or contributes research to the project.

Independent Reading Rubric

Use this rubric to periodically assess students' behaviors as independent readers.

Student Name: _____

Date: _____

CATEGORY	4	3	2	1
Frequency of Independent Reading	Student reads for extended periods of times daily.	Student reads most days.	Student reads occasionally.	Student seldom reads independently.
Difficulty Level of Books Selected	Student chooses books at or beyond independent reading level.	Student chooses books at independent reading level.	Student chooses books at and below independent reading level.	Student chooses books below independent reading level.
Variety of Genres Represented in Independent Reading	Student chooses texts from a wide variety of genres.	Student is willing to try reading texts from a variety of genres.	Student does little experimentation in reading various genres.	Student does no experimentation with genres.
Completion of Books Started	Student completes most books initiated independently and completes class reading.	Student completes many of the texts initiated independently and completes class reading.	Student completes less than half of the reading initiated independently and completes some of the class reading assignments.	Students fails to complete many books chosen independently and read as a class.

Writing Rubrics

Share with students these rubrics for expository, persuasive, and narrative writing. Remind students that:

- **expository writing** relates information.
- **persuasive writing** tries to convince readers of something.
- **narrative writing** tells a story.

Encourage students to add points to these rubrics to guide their writing. Extra space is provided in each rubric.

CATEGORY	4	3	2	1
Expository Writing	* My paper is well-developed. I have more than enough information to inform the reader about the topic. The information is presented clearly, with many details. * I have a clear pattern of organization. I use the same pattern throughout the writing. * I thought about the audience. * I frequently use language choices to maintain a style or a tone.	* My paper is fairly well-developed and I have enough information to inform the reader about the topic. The information is presented clearly, and there are some details about the topic. * I have a pattern of organization, and I try to stick to it. * I thought about the audience. * I use language choices to maintain a style or a tone.	* My paper has a small amount of information. The information does not clearly explain the topic. * I used details, but they may be the wrong details or they may not help to explain the topic. * I thought about the audience. * I do not have a clear style or tone.	* I did not tell enough about the topic. * I have only a few details. * It's hard to follow the organization. * I may not address the intended audience. * I do not have any style or tone.

CATEGORY	4	3	2	1
Persuasive Writing	* My stand on the issue is clear. * Numerous specific details support my stand. * My organization is logical. * I understand the type of audience I am writing for, and I use language that makes sense for persuasive writing. * I thought about my audience and how to persuade them.	* My stand on the issue is clear. * I have chosen enough specific details to support my stand. * My organization is logical. It strays only a little. * I use some persuasive language. * I have included ideas that will persuade my audience.	* My stand on the issue could be clearer. * There are some details, but they are general or may not really help to explain my position. * I tried to organize, but my writing jumps around. * I tried to understand the audience I was writing for. * I needed to use more persuasive language.	* I do not present a stand on an issue. * I have few details. * I have no real pattern of organization. * I did not try to write for the audience. * I used little persuasive language.

CATEGORY	4	3	2	1
Narrative Writing	* My paper is well-developed and complete. * I have a clear organization that makes sense for telling a story. * I meet the audience's needs. * I used language that makes sense for narrative writing.	* My paper has gaps or uneven parts. * I have an order that makes sense for telling a story. * I tried to meet the audience's needs. * I use language that for the most part makes sense for narrative writing.	* I tried to develop my ideas, but the paper is not whole or complete. * My order may get off track. * I tried to understand the audience I was writing for. * Not all my language "works" for narrative writing.	* I did not develop the ideas in a logical way. * My order is confusing. * My audience may not understand my ideas. * My language choices do not help tell the story.